LET'S CELEBRATE
Volume Two
More Assemblies for Special Occasions

By the same author:
Let's Celebrate

LET'S CELEBRATE
Volume Two
More Assemblies for Special Occasions

by

DIANA MORGAN

MOWBRAY
LONDON & OXFORD

Copyright © Diana Morgan 1986

ISBN 0 264 67091 4

First published 1986
by A. R. Mowbray & Co. Ltd,
Saint Thomas House, Becket Street,
Oxford, OX1 1SJ

Typeset by Acorn Bookwork, Salisbury, Wilts
Printed in Great Britain by Biddles Ltd, Guildford, Surrey

British Library Cataloguing in Publication Data

Morgan, Diana, *1931–*
    Let's celebrate.
    Vol. 2. More assemblies for special
    occasions
    1. Schools—Exercises and recreations
    I. Title
    377'.1   LB3015
    ISBN 0-264-67091-4

TO JOHN, HUGH and CLARE

ACKNOWLEDGEMENTS

Unless otherwise indicated, all Scripture quotations are from the Good News Bible, © American Bible Society, 1966, 1971, 1976, published by the Bible Societies and Collins.

Collects and prayers reproduced from The Alternative Service Book 1980 are copyright and reproduced with permission of the Central Board of Finance of the Church of England.

Extracts from the Book of Common Prayer of 1662 and the Authorized King James Version of the Bible, which are Crown Copyright in the United Kingdom, are reproduced by permission of Eyre & Spottiswoode (Publishers) Limited, Her Majesty's Printers, London.

Extracts from *The Rule of St Benedict*, translated by Justin McCann, are reproduced by permission of Sheed & Ward, London.

An extract from *Cider with Rosie* by Laurie Lee, first published by the Hogarth Press 1959 and © Laurie Lee 1959, is reproduced by permission of Chatto & Windus: The Hogarth Press.

Extracts from *Windows onto God* by Robert Runcie are quoted by kind permission of SPCK.

Extracts from *Four Prophets* by J. B. Phillips and *Surprised by Joy* by C. S. Lewis are reproduced by kind permission of Fontana Paperbacks.

Extracts from Her Majesty the Queen's speech on the evening of her coronation from *Times Coronation Supplement*, June 1953, and from Pope John Paul II's speech at Coventry in 1982 from *The Times*, are © Times Newspapers Ltd and are reproduced by permission of Robin Mead, TNL Syndication Department.

Unless otherwise stated, the Scripture quotations contained herein are from the Revised Standard Version of the Bible, copyrighted © 1946, 1952, 1971 by the Division of Christian Education of the National Council of the Churches of Christ in the USA and are used by permission. All rights reserved.

Extracts from *The Divine Office: the Liturgy of the Hours according to the Roman Rite*, published by William Collins, Sons and Co. Ltd, are reproduced by permission of the Hierarchies of Australia, England, Wales and Ireland.

Extracts from *Early Christian Writings*, translated by Maxwell Staniforth (Penguin Classics, 1968), pp. 158, 160, copyright © Maxwell Staniforth, 1968, are reprinted by permission of Penguin Books Ltd.

Extracts from *Passover* (Living Festivals Series), by Lynne Scholefield, are reproduced by permission of Religious and Moral Education Press.

Extracts from *The Life of St Francis* by G. K. Chesterton are reproduced by permission of A. P. Watt Ltd on behalf of Miss D. E. Collins.

A quotation from Gilbert Shaw: *A Pilgrim's Book of Prayers*, 1970, is reproduced with permission from the publishers, SLG Press, Convent of the Incarnation, Fairacres, Oxford.

An extract from 'Journey of the Magi' from *Collected Poems 1909–62* by T. S. Eliot is reproduced by permission of Faber and Faber Limited.

An extract from *For the Fallen* (September 1914) by Laurence Binyon is reproduced by permission of Mrs Nicolete Gray and the Society of Authors on behalf of the Laurence Binyon Estate.

CONTENTS

AUTUMN TERM

1. BEGINNINGS

This assembly was written with a new first-year class in mind. Working together quickly dispelled the strangeness of being in a new school and helped to develop a sense of belonging.

You will need: Two Readers
Cards which can be read from the back of the hall as follows:

(i)   Letter A
(ii) $1 + 1 = 2$
(iii)   Note A on the treble clef
(iv)   Once upon a time
(v)   On your marks
(vi)   Get set
(vii)   Go
(viii) January
(ix)   Picture of a chicken

A flower pot
Packet of seeds
An egg

Music: *The Teddy Bears' Picnic*

MUSIC – (Introduction)

READER 1   At the start of a new school year we are thinking about beginnings. Here comes the beginning of the alphabet.

(Continue music – first four bars of tune)

Enter child holding letter 'A'

(During bars 3 and 4, march across stage into position)

READER 2   All reading and writing starts here.

1

READER 1   And here comes the beginning of arithmetic.

                    (*Continue music – next four bars*)

                    Enter two children holding sign '1 + 1 = 2'

READER 2   All maths starts here.

READER 1   And here comes the beginning of music.

                    (*Continue music – next two bars*)

                    Enter child holding sign of note A in the treble clef

READER 2   No orchestra can begin without an A.

READER 1   Here comes the beginning of all the best stories.

                    Enter child with 'Once Upon a Time'

                    (*Continue music – next two bars*)

                    (*At this point extra children, according to the number available, sitting along the front of the stage can read famous openings, e.g. 'Once upon a time there were three bears'; the opening of Peter Rabbit, etc.*)

READER 2   Here comes the beginning of all the best races.

                    Enter three sporting types in games kit and signs saying 'On your marks, Get Set, Go'

                    (*Continue music – last four bars*)

READER 1   Then there's the beginning of a new year.

                    Enter child with January sign

                    (*Repeat first four bars of tune*)

READER 2   And the beginning of plants and flowers.

                    Enter two children with flower pot and packet of seeds

                    (*Next four bars of music*)

READER 1   And then the great question 'Which came first, the chicken or the egg?'

                    Enter two children, one with an egg, the other with a picture of a chicken – or dressed as a chicken

                    (*Next four bars of music*)

READER 2	And how did the world begin?
READER 1	We don't know yet, but we hope to by the time we are in the sixth form.

(Last four bars of tune)

READER 1	Now a question for you all. Can anybody remember how the Bible starts?
ALL	'In the beginning God . . .' (AV)
READER 1	And that's really the message of this Assembly – In the beginning *God*.
READER 2	So let's ask him to help us as we make a new beginning not only to this day but also to the whole school year.
Let us pray:	Almighty God, As we come before you at the beginning of the day, we ask your blessing on each one of us. Strengthen those of us new to the school, sustain those returning for another year, and grant that all our new beginnings may lead us ever closer to you, through Jesus Christ our Lord.

Hymn: Lord of all hopefulness

2. MICHAELMAS – 29 September

A few years ago a girl of thirteen wrote in an examination '29 September is Mickey Mouse day'. It gave me a laugh at the time but made me wonder what other strange things you half-believe and half-hear in lessons. So let's make it clear at the outset – today is Michaelmas Day as in Michaelmas daisies, which bloom at this time of the year, and it has nothing to do with Mr Disney. It is the feast of St Michael and all holy angels.

What are angels? I think most of us are conditioned to reply 'Angels are messengers' without giving too much thought to the question. Yet I suspect that deep down, if we were pushed, we should have to confess to having a hazy picture of a fair-haired mortal in a long nightgown with feathers growing from her shoulder-blades. Our

3

earliest school memories probably include the school nativity play. Were *you* ever an angel? – dressed in a sheet with wobbly wings made of bent wire and crêpe paper? Is this where that mental picture of angels starts? People probably thought you looked an angel in those days! But that is not how the Bible portrays angels. Listen to this:

Then war broke out in heaven. Michael and his angels fought against the dragon, who fought back with his angels; but the dragon was defeated, and he and his angels were not allowed to stay in heaven any longer. The huge dragon was thrown out – that ancient serpent, called the Devil, or Satan, that deceived the whole world. He was thrown down to earth, and all his angels with him.

(GNB, Rev. 12.7–9)

That's the archangel Michael throwing Satan and his devils out of heaven. Not much of the lady in a nightie with wobbly wings about him. Michael is the archangel of action – of battles in God's cause.

Remember Gabriel who was sent to announce to Zechariah that his wife, Elizabeth, would have a son in her old age? That baby grew up to be John the Baptist. It was Gabriel too who came to Mary with the most important announcement in history – the coming of Jesus. And to both Zechariah and Mary Gabriel had to say 'Fear not' – so awesome was this close presence of God's messenger.

Medieval men used to speculate about how many angels could dance on a pin. At least they hadn't so domesticated these spiritual beings that they had destroyed all sense of wonder and awe at them. I'm not decrying those kindergarten angels. We all have to start somewhere. What I am trying to say is that our understanding of spiritual things needs to grow up as we grow up.

'When I was a child, my speech, feelings, and thinking were all those of a child; now that I am a man, I have no more use for childish ways.'

(GNB, I. Corinth. 13.11)

says St Paul. So, it's fun for the Brown children to befriend a bear on Paddington station when they are of an age to see no difference between him and themselves. It is natural for them to go on loving him once they have grown up – I still love my bear. But, if we are to grow into sane adults, it is essential that we should acknowledge the difference between Paddington Bear and a real bear escaped from the zoo, because the real bear is powerful enough to pick us up and hug *us* rather than the other way round.

And so to guardian angels. Do you know that we each have a guardian angel? Jesus, speaking of little children, says

'See that you don't despise any of these little ones. Their angels in heaven, I tell you, are always in the presence of my Father in heaven.'
(GNB, Matt. 18.10)

And the psalmist tells us,

God will put his angels in charge of you
to protect you wherever you go.
They will hold you up with their hands
to keep you from hurting your feet on the stones.
(GNB, Psalm 91.11–12)

So God has provided us with angels to guard us and guide us. What could be more wonderful than that? At one end of the scale we are given a vision of 'ten thousand times ten thousand, and thousands of thousands' (AV, Rev. 5.11) worshipping before the throne of God and yet these messengers of God are right here with us now, guiding us and protecting us. They are much more wonderful than our limited mental pictures of them allow us to understand. So let St Bernard have the last word:

Though we are children and the road that lies ahead of us is so long, and not only long but dangerous, what have we to fear with such guardians? They cannot be vanquished, nor led astray, still less can they lead us astray, these beings who guard us in all our ways. They are faithful, they are wise, they are powerful; what have we to fear? Let us but follow them and cling to them, and we shall abide in the shadow of the Almighty.
(Sermon 12 on Psalm 90 from the *Divine Office, Roman Rite*, p. 307*)

Let us pray: Lord God of hosts,
in your all-wise plan
you assign to angels and to men
the services they have to render you.
Grant that the angels who adore you in heaven,
may protect us here on earth.
We make our prayer through our Lord Jesus
Christ.
(*Divine Office, Roman Rite*, p. 300*)

Hymn: Ye holy angels bright

3. ST FRANCIS OF ASSISI – 4 October

A simple mime of two scenes in which a whole class can be involved.

You will need: Francis
A beggar
Market crowd
Variable number of cloth merchants
Variable number of friends to build church
Pietro Bernadone
Bishop
Two Readers

Music: Grieg's *Peer Gynt Suite*. It is simple to tape musical extracts of the correct length in the order in which they will be needed.

Narrative can be 'live' or – easier for rehearsal – taped.

TEACHER Today's saint, St Francis, has perhaps suffered more than most from sentimental stories. Pictures of him are likely to show a slim young man clad in the familiar brown Franciscan habit with a knotted rope around his waist, a bird sitting on one finger, a pink-eared rabbit gazing adoringly at him from the ground, primroses smiling at his feet and wolves and lambs gambolling side by side all around him. Such pictures present a travesty of the truth yet how can we, in ten minutes, set you right?

St Francis' life was full of paradoxes – that means things which are apparently contradictory to the point of seeming absurd. He sometimes seemed crazy yet was more sane than the sanest of men. His whole being danced with joy, yet he sought hardships. He was a lover – in love with Christ – and our own Shakespeare tells us

'the lunatic, the lover and the poet
are of imagination all compact.'
A Midsummer Night's Dream, Act 5 sc. 1)

Your friend may seem slightly off her head when she falls in love – and yet she's fun to be with,

6

more alive, positive, joyful than normal. So it was with St Francis.

Our first scene is in the market place of Assisi.

Curtain

(Tape: Norwegian Bridal Procession)

READER   Francis Bernadone, the son of a wealthy cloth merchant, is selling expensive velvets and embroidery from a market stall. Nearby is a fruit stall where melons, grapes and plums surmount piles of vegetables of all kinds. A happy, jostling crowd of people stroll in the sunshine. Housewives with their baskets pause to gossip, to taste the greengrocer's wares, selecting carefully or rejecting what he has to offer. Francis Bernadone's bales of cloth are too expensive for them but several rich merchants are deep in conversation with him, bargaining over the fine fabrics set out before them.

Weaving his way through the crowds comes a beggar, pathetic in his rags and pleading with the passers-by for alms. Some turn away from him, some ignore him. The greengrocer throws him an apple which he devours ravenously. Then he sidles up to Francis who is engrossed in his bargaining. He plucks at his sleeve. Francis turns absent-mindedly towards him, but returns to his bargaining. The beggar persists; Francis becomes more and more distraught between the two conversations and eventually turns his back on the beggar to complete his bargain. The beggar slinks away. When the merchants depart, Francis picks up a coin and looks round for the beggar. He is nowhere to be seen. Francis asks the crowd. Some shake their heads but one man points in the direction taken by the beggar. Francis returns to his stall, picks up all the money he has taken that day and hurries after the beggar.

Curtain – fade music

Enter beggar in front of curtain followed shortly by Francis

7

He catches up with him and hands the astonished man a bag of gold, shakes him warmly by the hand and vows before God that he will never again for the rest of his life refuse to help a poor man.

Exeunt

Later it was to be said of him 'His life was one riot of rash vows; of rash vows that turned out right'.
(*Life of St Francis* by G. K. Chesterton, ch. 3, p. 43)

Change music – Death of Aase

It became a habit with Francis to go to the ruined church of St Damian to pray before a beautiful crucifix. He was going through a difficult time. He had tried the life of a soldier and had gone into battle against the rival city of Perugia. He had been taken prisoner, had become very ill and, when the war was over and he returned home, he was listless, unsure of the path in life he should take.

One day as he prayed it seemed to him that the figure on the cross spoke to him.

READER 2 'Francis, do you not see that my church is in ruins? Go and restore it for me.'
(G. K. Chesterton, Ch. 4, p. 57)

Fade music

READER 1 No sooner said than done. There was nothing⁹ Francis liked better than action.

Curtain

Change music – In the Hall of the Mountain King

READER He gathered together some friends and they beavered away as fast as they could, finding stones, carrying them to the church, chiselling and banging for all they were worth. If you go to that church to this very day you can see where some of the stonework has obviously been done by not very experienced amateurs.

They needed money. Francis sold his horse and

8

then thought nothing of selling bales of his father's cloth and diverting the proceeds to his church repair scheme. After all, was not this God's work? His father didn't see it that way. He stormed and raged at his son who could not see that he had done anything wrong. After all, hadn't God told him to restore his church?

Pietro Bernadone brought in the bishop to reason with his son. The bishop told him it was stealing to use his father's money for his own schemes and that he could not do God's work by the devil's means. Still Francis couldn't agree. God had told him to restore his church and who was the bishop to stop him? Eventually, exasperated beyond endurance, he declared

READER 2   'Up to this time I have called Pietro Bernadone father, but now I am the servant of God. Not only the money but everything that can be called his I will restore to my father, even the very clothes he has given me.'

(G. K. Chesterton, Ch. 4, p. 59)

and one by one he stripped off his garments

Curtain

leaving them in a heap at his father's feet until he stood naked before him. It is said that the bishop put his own cloak around him to shield him and that Francis went off singing.

Fade music

And so, free from all material encumbrances, he set about living the life of the gospel literally. If anyone asked him for his shirt he gave him his coat as well. To those who smote him on one cheek, he offered also the other with words of love. When anyone asked for anything, he gave it to them. He carried the teaching of Christ to its logical conclusion and the world was transfixed.

Men wanted to join him and the whole amazing story of the founding of the Franciscan order began. This surely was the true meaning of the words God spoke to St Francis in the church of St Damian. The church – the whole people of God – was ready to be restored, recalled to the basic simplicity of Christ's teaching and the life of the saint was to show the way.

Pause – Change music – Prelude to Act 4 (Morning)

So what about those pictures of St Francis preaching to the birds? saving turtle-doves from the market and making nests for them with his own hands? converting the fierce wolf of Agobio who had been terrorizing the neighbourhood?

Legends of the saints abound with stories of shy creatures being drawn to the saint by his sanctity, but in the case of St Francis the legends tell us something more profound. Each of us is dear to God, created by one heavenly Father. So every creature from ant to elephant is my brother or sister. Does this affect the way I treat created things? Think about it.

Conclude music

And now let us pray the prayer of St Francis:

Lord, make me an instrument of thy peace,
where there is hatred let me sow love;
where there is injury, pardon;
where there is doubt, faith;
where there is despair, hope;
where there is darkness, light;
and where there is sadness, joy.
Lord, that I may seek to console rather than to be
    consoled;
to understand, rather than to be understood;
to love rather than to be loved.
For it is in giving that we receive;
in self-forgetfulness that we find our true selves,
in forgiving that we are forgiven,
in dying that we are raised up to life everlasting.

10

And our hymn is an adaptation of a great poem written by the saint:

All creatures of our God and king

4. HARVEST FESTIVAL

You will need a piece of beech mast, opening but preferably with the nuts still intact and/or a conker visible but still inside its case.

Hymn: We plough the fields and scatter

What a wonderful display we have for the harvest this morning. Be sure to thank your parents for their generosity. Year by year we gather to thank God for the harvest and do what we can to share his bounty with other people. But it's all too easy to be so preoccupied with singing our thanks to God that we forget to thank Mum who has raided the larder or the garden to help us bring together all these fruits of the earth.

Now obviously our first thought on an occasion like this, when we look at all these tins and packets – to say nothing of the fruit and vegetables – is thankfulness that the larder is going to be full and that there is no need for us to go hungry this winter. We shall probably also think of some of the famine-stricken parts of the world and may be moved to give money to one of the relief organizations as a way of sharing our own blessings with others. I hope so.

But are we really aware of our dependence on things beyond our control? Do you know that one-third of the world eats two-thirds of the world's food supply? We are rich enough to be able to afford to be greedy. If our apple harvest fails we can buy apples from overseas – or most of us can. I vividly remember once visiting a friend in a monastery which aimed at being self-sufficient. That year there had been a very poor apple crop and so the monks just had to go without. That makes you think of our dependence on things outside our control at a very practical level. One of the monks, looking on the bright side, explained that there had been a splendid crop of crab apples and that they were eating those instead. Bearing in mind that they had no sugar and were dependent on their bees to supply them

11

with sweetening, I wondered how he could be thankful in those circumstances. Yet St Paul tells us

'In the name of our Lord Jesus Christ, always give thanks for everything to God the Father.'
(GNB, Eph. 5.20)

So we give thanks for food. What else do we delight in at this season of the year? What about sight, taste, touch, sound, smell? – our senses.

Look at the riot of colour in this display. Supposing God had made the world black and white instead of coloured? Can we not delight in colour and our ability to see and enjoy it? Then thank him for it.

Imagine your favourite taste. Is it fish fingers? Baked beans? Mars bars? Spinach? Coke? – but supposing God had made everything in the world taste the same? You might think it would have been lovely if it had been your favourite flavour. But supposing it had been one of *my* favourite flavours – sprouts?! Even if it had been your own favourite flavour, you might grow sick of it in three score years and ten. So let's thank God for the variety of tastes set out before us here.

Do you get the idea? Pause for a moment and think of the other senses for yourselves – touch – hearing – smell – and then let us thank God for giving us senses to use and enjoy.

Hymn: For the beauty of the earth

And now, before we close, as we look at all these fruits of the earth, let us think for a moment about our own lives and whether they are fruitful. Do you remember that passage in the fourth gospel where Jesus says,

'I am the true vine, and my Father is the vinedresser. Every branch of mine that bears no fruit, he takes away, and every branch that does bear fruit he prunes, that it may bear more fruit. You are already made clean by the word which I have spoken to you. Abide in me, and I in you. As the branch cannot bear fruit by itself, unless it abides in the vine, neither can you, unless you abide in me. I am the vine, you are the branches. He who abides in me, and I in him, he it is that bears much fruit, for apart from me you can do nothing.'
(RSV, John 15.1–5)

The fruit he is talking about is that list of fruits of the Spirit which St Paul gives us –

12

'love, joy, peace, patience, kindness, goodness, faithfulness, humility, and self-control'

(GNB, Gal. 5.22)

How are we to acquire them? Not through our own clever effort. How did these fruits in our display grow? Not through their own effort but through being open to God's gifts – 'the breezes and the sunshine and soft refreshing rain'. That's how we have to be. Look at this piece of beech mast. Can you see it? It's open with the little nuts – the fruit – ready to be spilled out. Or imagine a conker, still in its case but ready to burst out as the case splits. That's how we have to be. If we want to be *fruitful*, we have to be *open* – open to God's love which so warms us that we want to get out and share it instead of staying shut up inside ourselves.

So let's thank God for that love showered on us in such profusion. Then, as we recognize his bounty and become thankful for it, we in our turn will become richly fruitful through his grace.

Hymn: Come, ye thankful people, come

Let us pray: Almighty and everlasting God,
we offer you our hearty thanks
for your fatherly goodness and care
in giving us the fruits of the earth in their
seasons.
Give us grace to use them rightly,
to your glory,
for our own well-being,
and for the relief of those in need;
through Jesus Christ our Lord.
(ASB, Harvest thanksgiving collect, p. 890)

5. ONE WORLD WEEK

You will need a variable number of children who are prepared to say a few words to the assembly about relatives and friends who live in different parts of the world. Some of these, or others, can share in reading parts of the assembly, or it may be entirely teacher-led.

TEACHER   Do you know the term 'global village'? What do
you think it means? Apart from size, what are the
differences between living in a town and a village?
Think for a moment. . . .

There are lots of differences, of course, but one
which I am sure most of you will have thought of
is that in a village everybody knows everybody
else. That's why some corners of even a large city
like London can have the character of village life.
If you yourself live in a village, you may well hate
having the neighbours knowing what you are up
to and you may long for the anonymity of a town.
But it can be terrifying to live in a town where
nobody knows you and you have no individual to
turn to when troubles come – as they will come to
all of us at some time in our lives.

As you approach London by rail, particularly
from an easterly direction, you will pass tower
blocks of flats which were built to rehouse families
after the bombing of the Second World War. To
the unthinking it seems a good idea to build up
into the sky when land for houses is scarce. You
hear people on trains saying 'What a marvellous
view there must be from the top'. Well, I've been
on the twenty-sixth floor of one of those tower
blocks. The view *is* wonderful – if you can bear to
look down. The River Thames is like a silver
snake far below and people in the street seem like
ants. The lift wasn't working the day of my visit so
there was a great stillness – and a terrifying sense
of isolation. There was the life of the world going
on down below – far, far away – and I was cut off
from it up in the sky with nobody to know or care
what happened to me. Supposing I had been
handicapped in some way – old, with arthritis,
young and unemployed with no part to play in
that life bustling below? What would I have felt
like? None of those tiny ants rushing around
down below even realized I was there. They certainly wouldn't have heard if I had called. I might
just as well not have not existed.

Compare that with life in a village. There I

14

might well be regarded as a nuisance, a tiresome old woman forever complaining about the younger generation, but I would be known and people would notice if I were starving.

Come back to that idea of the 'global village'. Forget sheer numbers for a moment and think about other members of the world community in which we all live.

As many children as possible to give a brief idea of the way of life of relatives in as wide a variety of countries as possible

So most of us have people we care about in other parts of the world. Think now about the twelve *million* children under the age of five who will die of hunger this year. Are we going to be like one of the ants twenty-six floors down rushing about on our own business with no time to spare for anyone else? Or are we going to notice them crying out for help? Are we going to hide behind the anonymity of town life or are we prepared to behave in the world as we would in our own village? – not necessarily being uncritical (think of the gossip in a village!) – but being prepared to help.

READER   Rich countries of the world make up less than a third of the world's population but we eat two-thirds of the world's food supply. The world produces enough cereal to provide everyone in the world with three thousand calories a day.

TEACHER   Those of you who have been on a reducing diet will know that, in order to lose weight, it is desirable to cut your intake of food to provide one thousand calories. Unless we are doing very heavy work, we don't need more than fifteen hundred.

READER   So, if the earth produces three thousand calories for each of us, why are five hundred million people suffering from malnutrition?

READER   One-third of all that cereal is fed to cattle to provide meat, milk, butter and cheese for us, the rich of the world. *We* can afford to pay for it so

15

people in poor countries have to go without the grain which could save lives.

TEACHER Is that what life in a village is like? Have you heard of butter mountains? The destruction of bumper harvests to protect farmers against falling prices? Two million cauliflowers being destroyed – having poison poured over them to make sure the poor (or the rich) don't sneak out and help themselves for nothing? When we read that in India the population of a whole village was wiped out by disease because hunger drove someone to eat cow dung, it is time we questioned our own comfortable lives.

READER It is not a new problem. Amos, in the eighth century BC, had this to say,

Alas for the complacent ones in Zion . . .
You who lie on beds of ivory,
And sprawl upon your couches,
Eating choice lamb and farm-fed veal.
Who croon to the music of the harp,
And compose melodies as though you were
    David himself!
You who drink wine by the bowl-full,
And anoint yourselves with the finest oils.
But never a thought do you spare
For the terrible miseries of Joseph!
(J. B. Phillips, *Four Prophets* Amos 6.1a, 4–6,
Fontana)

TEACHER You may well say, 'I can't do anything about it. That's Economics and only governments can work out that kind of thing.' But democratic governments are elected by people. They need our votes so we *can* make our views felt. Some of you will have the vote quite soon now. Are you going to take note of what the different political parties are prepared to do for the under-privileged in our global village or are you only going to notice what they promise to do for you? The poor are like the persons isolated on the twenty-sixth floor with no hope of drawing atten-

16

tion to themselves but knowing there is a thriving life going on somewhere far away.

There is something you can do right now. A few years ago pressure was brought to bear on our government to *increase* our nation's giving to one per cent of our Gross National Product. That means 1p in every £ to be spent on aid. Those efforts failed. It was decided we couldn't afford giving on that scale. People would not be prepared to go without something else. Would *you*? How much pocket money do you get? 50p? £1? Would you be prepared to give away one per cent – 1p in every pound? What about Saturday jobs? Do you earn £5? Could you spare 5p? Do you do a paper round? How much do you earn? Would you give 1p out of every pound? This is *not* a matter of charitable giving – sparing a coin for a good cause now and again. It needs to be organized – to become a way of life. Just for this week – One World Week – we are going to help you start by having a jar on a table as you come in to assembly in which you can put what you want to give. Now *don't* go home to Mum and say 'Please can I have some money for One World Week?' If this isn't your own offering, we don't want it. And the giving is entirely voluntary. Think it out for yourself. Next week, when we know how much money we have, we'll ask forms which charity they would like the money to go to and take a vote. Possibly there won't be a great deal of money this year, but remember One World Week comes round every year and it's the *habit* of thinking of ourselves as members of a global village that we are trying to cultivate. Keep up your 1p in the pound for fifty-two weeks and *next* year we should have enough money really to save lives. We live in a global village and the people in undeveloped countries have a claim on our love.

Let us pray: Almighty God, whose only Son, our Saviour Jesus Christ,
taught us to call you Father,

We remember before you our brothers and
    sisters throughout
the world who are in need:
Open our hearts to show them your love through
    our care
and help us to be generous in sharing your
    blessings with all men.

Hymn: Far round the world

6. ALL SAINTS – 1 November

No sun – no moon!
No morn – no noon –
No dawn – no dusk – no proper time of day –
    No sky – no earthly view –
    No distance looking blue –
No road – no street – no 't'other side the way' –
    No end to any Row –
    No indications where the Crescents go –
    No top to any steeple –
No recognitions of familiar people –
    No courtesies for showing 'em –
    No knowing 'em! –
No travelling at all – no locomotion,
No inkling of the way – no notion –
    'No go' – by land or ocean –
    No mail – no post –
No news from any foreign coast –
No Park – no Ring – no afternoon gentility –
    No company – no nobility –
No warmth, no cheerfulness, no healthful ease,
    No comfortable feel in any member –
No shade, no shine, no butterflies, no bees,
    No fruits, no flowers, no leaves, no birds, –
        November!

(Thomas Hood, *No*)

18

Is that how *you* feel about November? For many of us it is not a month with particularly happy associations. The rich colour and golden sunlight of autumn are behind us. Ahead lie months of chilly, barren living. For some, O-level retakes are beginning to loom; Christmas is still a long way off. Admittedly we shall be having fireworks in a few days' time, but, unless I'm much mistaken, on that day you will be given a serious and rather deflating warning of the dangers of that particular celebration and undoubtedly on 6 November we shall hear of people who have lost their sight through accidents. No – November is not a merry month.

And yet here we are on its first day invited to share in the great Church festival of All Saints. Many of you, I am sure, were celebrating Hallowe'en last night. Did you know what it meant? Those 'hallows' whose 'eve' you were celebrating are the saints. Do you know why you dressed up as witches and ghosts and made turnip lanterns? Those celebrations are really part of old pagan customs – and great fun they are. There's no need to be terribly serious about the reasons for such games as 'apple bobbing' and 'trick or treat'.

But what about All Saints? Listen to St John's account of his great vision at the end of the Bible,

'After this I looked, and behold, a great multitude which no man could number, from every nation, from all tribes and peoples and tongues, standing before the throne and before the Lamb, clothed in white robes, with palm branches in their hands, and crying out with a loud voice, 'Salvation belongs to our God who sits upon the throne, and to the Lamb!' And all the angels stood round the throne and round the elders and the four living creatures, and they fell upon their faces before the throne and worshipped God, saying, 'Amen! Blessing and glory and wisdom and thanksgiving and honour and power and might be to our God for ever and ever! Amen.'

(RSV, Rev. 7.9–12)

Who are they? They are the countless men and women down the ages who have stood firmly by their loyalty to Christ in great events and small. People like St Paul, who travelled the world with the good news of redemption and endured incredible hardships for his faith; people like St Thérèse of Lisieux, who stayed put in her convent and who found one of her hardships was to endure the sister sitting next to her incessantly rattling the beads of her rosary – one of the small things which could drive you mad, yet through that experience the saint acquired heroic patience; people like St Francis of Assisi who gave away all possessions and roamed freely at God's command;

19

others like St Benedict who founded monasteries which, apart from being power houses of prayer, preserved learning through a troubled period of world history. And still others – countless others – whose names are known only to God. Saints are fully-fledged Christians and we are *all* called to be saints. 'Be ye perfect', said Jesus. Rather depressing really – like the gloomy month of November – when you think how far most of us ordinary people have to go to reach that particular winning post.

And then comes All Saints Day and we realize, not only that it *can* be done through God's grace, but also that all those saints are our brothers and sisters in Christ. *They* have reached the goal and there they are cheering *us* on. You know the effect on Sports Day of hearing your House cheering for you. Maybe the relay is just about over and you are a whole length behind everyone else. There doesn't seem much point in going on and then suddenly you hear your name, you hear friends cheering you on and somehow you find the courage to go on and finish.

It is the same in the spiritual world. We praise God for the saints. They add their prayers to ours. One of them, St Augustine, put it like this when he was still living his life in *this* world,

How happy will be our shout of Alleluia there, how carefree, how secure from any adversary, where there is no enemy, where no friend perishes. There praise is offered to God, and here, too, but here it is by men who are anxious, there by men who are free from care, here by men who must die, there by men who will live for ever. Here praise is offered in hope, there by men who enjoy the reality, here by men who are pilgrims on the way, there by men who have reached their own country. So, brethren, let us sing Alleluia, not in the enjoyment of heavenly rest, but to sweeten our toil. Sing as travellers sing along the road: but keep on walking. Solace your toil by singing – do not yield to idleness. Sing but keep on walking. What do I mean by 'walking'? I mean, press on from good to better. The apostle says there are some who go from bad to worse. But if you press on, you keep on walking. Go forward then in virtue, in true faith and right conduct. Sing up – and keep on walking.

(Sermon 256 quoted in *Divine Office, Roman Rite,* p. 824 – Week 34 of the year)

Let us pray: Almighty, ever-living God,
we are celebrating with joy
the triumph of your grace in all the saints.
With so vast a multitude praying for us,

20

may we receive from you
the fulness of mercy we have always desired.
We make our prayer through our Lord.
(Concluding prayer for All Saints Day, *Divine
Office, Roman Rite*, p. 364*)

Hymn: For all the saints

7. FRIDAY BEFORE REMEMBRANCE SUNDAY

Music: 'Nimrod' from Elgar's *Enigma Variations*

This week we have been buying poppies because next Sunday is
Remembrance Day. A few years ago people used to wonder whether
there was any future for the annual service of Remembrance at the
cenotaph in Whitehall. After all, only one in ten of our population
was born before the First World War and well under half were born
before the Second World War. How were we to honour the dead in a
way which would have meaning for young people without detracting
from the traditions which mean so much to those who experienced
the wars?

Then came the Falklands conflict. Suddenly a new generation was
brought face to face night after night with pictures of the horror, the
hurt, the courage and the pity of war. Everyone again knows of
someone who has been affected by it. And so, on Sunday, the nation
will unite with the Queen and the statesmen as they honour the dead
at the cenotaph and express the gratitude of the living for the lives
which have been sacrificed for us.

Do you know what the word cenotaph means? It comes from two
Greek words – kenos, meaning empty, and taphos, meaning tomb.
It's a monument to people whose bodies are elsewhere. Any of you
who have been through northern France will know too well where
many of these dead lie buried. Military cemeteries abound with their
rows and rows of plain crosses – a sobering reminder of the bat-
tlefields of this century. In 1920 the body of an unknown soldier was
buried in Westminster Abbey, among the greatest men and women
our country has ever produced, and the King – our present Queen's
grandfather – unveiled the cenotaph in Whitehall. Each year since
then, on the Sunday nearest to 11 November, which marked the end

of the First World War, the world has paused at 11 o'clock to reflect during two minutes of silence on what it is all about. There was a time when all traffic stopped for those two minutes and a great hush fell. Nowadays many no longer bother. If you hear the maroons on Sunday, and particularly if you are in the company of older people to whom this is a very moving moment, pause in what you are doing and reflect, and allow them the peace to do so too.

How do you reflect? What are you to reflect about? Listen to this poem. Maybe it will give you food for thought. We'll keep silence for just one minute at the end to give it time to sink in. It was written by Wilfred Owen who was killed just seven days before the end of the First World War. He is looking at a dead comrade and muses on the fact that until this particular morning the sun had always gently awakened his friend as it awakens the life in all growing things. Surely, he thinks, if anyone knows how to restore his friend to life, 'the kind old sun will know'. The poem is called 'Futility', which means 'Uselessness'.

Move him into the sun –
Gently its touch awoke him once.
At home, whispering of fields unsown.
Always it woke him, even in France,
Until this morning and this snow.
If anything might rouse him now
The kind old sun will know.

Think how it wakes the seeds, –
Woke, once, the clays of a cold star.
Are limbs, so dear-achieved, are sides,
Full-nerved – still warm – too hard to stir?
Was it for this the clay grew tall?
– O what made fatuous sunbeams toil
To break earth's sleep at all?

Now just think quietly about that poem. Dwell for a moment on why it is called 'Futility'.

At the end of the Falklands conflict a great service of thanksgiving was arranged in St Paul's Cathedral. Many expected it to be a triumphal celebration – 'Rule Britannia' and all that – when suddenly the whole occasion was lifted to a higher plane by the address of the Archbishop of Canterbury, Dr Robert Runcie. He began certainly with thanksgiving for the courage and endurance of those who fought in that conflict. He reminded the congregation that there were many present who were mourning the loss of someone they loved. He went on to point out that the Argentinians were also mourning their dead and said,

'The parent who comes mourning the loss of a son may find here consolation, but also a spirit which enlarges our compassion to include all those Argentinian parents who have lost sons.'

(quoted in *Windows onto God*, SPCK, p. 110)

Our neighbours are indeed like us,' he said.

(Ibid, p. 109)

Is this something you could think about during the two minutes' silence on Sunday? 'Our neighbours' – all those foreigners to whom we give rude names, those we dislike in this school as well as those we like – 'are indeed like us'.

Or one last suggestion. During his visit to this country, the Pope went to Coventry where he spoke words which will be remembered for many years to come. He said,

'War should belong to the tragic past, to history. It should find no place on humanity's agenda for the future.'

That's where you come in. Think first of Wilfred Owen's poem, 'Futility'. Then remember the failures of my generation which have produced conflict and finally resolve that war 'should find no place on humanity's agenda for the future'. Then you needn't be stuck for food for reflection during the two minutes' silence on Sunday.

For our prayer let's use the well-known poem by Laurence Binyon which has become traditional at this season.

'They shall not grow old, as we that are left grow old:
Age shall not weary them, nor the years condemn.
At the going down of the sun and in the morning
We will remember them.'

(*For the Fallen*, September 1914)

Hymn: Dear Lord and father of mankind

23

kx.

8. ST HILDA – 17 November

You will need:	Two Readers Caedmon Variable number of banqueters (two speaking parts) Angel Bailiff A few monks/nuns Small harp/lyre A bell
Music:	Vaughan Williams' *Fantasia on a Theme of Thomas Tallis*

READER 1 This morning we want you to come back with us in imagination to the kingdom of Northumbria around the time of the Council of Whitby which was held in the year 663.

READER 2 In Whitby there was an unusual monastery. It was mixed – monks and nuns. That in itself was not all that unusual. They lived in separate buildings but joined together for worship in the chapel eight times a day. What made Whitby unusual was that there was a woman in charge. Her name was Hilda. You might think her election to the office of abbess was the start of Women's Lib. But you would be mistaken. There wasn't much liberation about St Hilda.

READER 1 She was a remarkable administrator and a woman of great wisdom. The story we are going to tell you about her today concerns a cowherd in her monastery by the name of Caedmon.

Music

Curtain

(Banquet in progress. Men seated in a semi-circle. Murmur of voices. Caedmon is seated near the front and beside him one of the banqueters, holding the harp, is finishing his story.)

24

BANQUETER 1   . . . and as the hero cut off the monster's head, his thanes roared their approval and sang the praises of their lord.

(*Applause*)

He gets up, crosses the stage and hands the harp to the man opposite.

B/ BANQUETER 2   Mine, oh friends, is a very different song. I sing of Creation.

(*He strikes the harp, proclaiming 'Hwaet'*)

CAEDMON   (*aside*) Would that I could sing. My heart misses a beat each time the harp is passed around. I would die of shame if it came to me and I remained silent.

BANQUETER 2   In the beginning God created the heaven and the earth. And the earth was without form, and void; and darkness was upon the face of the deep. And the Spirit of God moved upon the face of the waters. And God said, Let there be light: and there was light. And God saw the light, that it was good: and God divided the light from the darkness. And God called the light Day, and the darkness he called Night. And the evening and the morning were the first day.

(AV, Gen. 1.1–5)

CAEDMON   Beautiful – but, oh dear God, I fear my turn must come. I dare not stay. I am ashamed of my cowardice but go I must.

(*He slips out*)

BANQUETER 2   And God said, Let there be a firmament in the midst of the waters, and let it divide the waters from the waters.

(AV, Gen. 1.6)

Curtain as he is speaking

Music – gradually fade, reader speaking above it

READER 1   That night Caedmon lay in the cowshed.

Curtain – fade music completely

25

CAEDMON (*propped on one arm*) 'In the beginning God created the heaven and the earth.' What a wonderful story that was! My heart was ready to burst with joy at the wonder of God's creation and yet, for lack of training, I had to remain dumb.

Enter angel

ANGEL Caedmon, sing me something.

CAEDMON I don't know how to sing and that is why I have left the banquet and come here because I don't know how to sing.

ANGEL Nevertheless, sing me something.

CAEDMON What shall I sing?

ANGEL Sing me of Creation.

Music quietly. Caedmon speaks above it

CAEDMON Now we must praise the guardian of the heavenly kingdom,
The might of the Creator and his powers of insight –
The work of the father of glory

Pause – music

So he, the eternal king, the holy creator
instituted the first beginning of every wondrous thing.
He first created for the children of earth
Heaven for a roof.
Afterwards the eternal king, almighty Lord
Created the world, the earth for mankind.

Music runs on – then silence

CAEDMON (*in wonder*) Praise God! Praise his Holy Name. He has taken away my affliction. He has granted me the joy of praising his name in song. Oh my Lord – praise be to thee forever.

A bell tolls

CAEDMON Day is starting in the community. I must tell them what has happened.

Curtain

Caedmon enters in front of curtain, crosses stage and meets bailiff.

26

CAEDMON   Master, may I have a word with you?
BAILIFF   What is it, my man? Trouble with the cattle?
CAEDMON   No, sir. I hardly know how to tell you. I wonder if
                I might see my lady abbess. A miracle has hap-
                pened. She would understand.
BAILIFF   *You* see the abbess? What has the cowherd to say
                to my lady abbess?
CAEDMON   Only this, master. That our Lord has given *me* the
                gift of song. Please – *please* – let me tell reverend
                mother herself. Let her judge whether a miracle
                has happened.
BAILIFF   *You* – the gift of song? I don't believe it. I've
                noticed how you always slip away after the meal
                when the entertainment starts. I guessed it was
                because you feared to be caught out.
CAEDMON   Not any more. Please let me tell Mother Hilda.
BAILIFF   So be it. Come with me.

                Exeunt. Music

                Curtain

                Abbess Hilda sitting C. talking to another monk/
                nun.

ABBESS   Caedmon, you say? By all means. Bring him in.

                Enter Caedmon with bailiff. They bow

ABBESS   What's this I hear, Caedmon? Tell me in your
                own words.
CAEDMON   Reverend mother, for years it has been a great
                affliction to me that I could neither play nor sing
                in tune. Last night after the banquet when the
                entertainment started, I fled to the cowshed
                rather than risk being shamed before everyone by
                having to remain silent when the harp was passed
                to me. As I lay there, remembering the beautiful
                song of Creation I had heard, it seemed to me –
                whether I was awake or asleep I cannot say – that
                a stranger asked me to sing him something. When
                I said I did not know how to, he said, 'Neverthe-
                less sing me something' – and my lady, I *did*. It
                wasn't a dream. I can remember it all and sing it
                all still.
ABBESS   Then sing it to me now.

Music – as Caedmon starts – Curtain

READER 1   And Caedmon's song was the very first poem written in the ordinary English of ordinary people.

READER 2   St Hilda recognized the importance of Caedmon's gift. She encouraged him to become a monk and he was given every opportunity to learn all the monastery could teach him so that he could turn the well-loved stories into poetry and song. So, as we remember St Hilda today, let us also remember the cowherd Caedmon, our very first English poet. Without the help of the saint his gift might have been lost forever.

Let us pray: Father,
we praise and thank you for your gifts to
poets, musicians, artists and craftsmen of all
   kinds.
Through their insights may we be led to you,
the source of all holiness.
We ask it through our Lord Jesus Christ.

Hymn: Praise the Lord, ye heavens adore him

or song of Caedmon ~ H.P.

9. ST HUGH – 17 November

You will need: Two Readers
King Henry II
Variable number of courtiers
Chancellor
Scribe (non-speaking part)
St Hugh
Variable number of citizens of Lincoln
   (five speaking parts)

Music: *Greensleeves*
Tape of bells or chime bars

READER 1 Have you heard of Lincoln's Inn in London? If you go to Lincoln's Inn Fields nowadays you will find a bandstand, possibly see people playing netball or tennis. Certainly there will be office workers strolling there in their lunch hour. The Royal College of Surgeons has its home there. So does the Imperial Cancer Research Fund. The gardens are bright with flowers – and I doubt if you would find anyone there strolling in the sunshine who could tell you why it is called *Lincoln*'s Inn Fields. They might point to the nearby Law Courts and explain to you about the Inns of Court. But why *Lincoln*'s Inn? Watch carefully and you will find out.

READER 2 We are going back to the days of Henry II. It is some years since his knights had murdered Archbishop Thomas à Becket in Canterbury cathedral. The king had lived to regret his rash words but had not altogether changed his character. As part of his penance he had undertaken to establish a monastery at Witham in Somerset and we see him now in London being confronted by some of the problems that had arisen.

Music – Curtain slowly

The king is seated, surrounded by courtiers. His chancellor stands before him. Fade music

HENRY But why? What's wrong? I don't understand the delay. When the king says 'Establish a monastery' he expects to be obeyed. I have long admired the sanctity of the Carthusians. It is good that they should have a house in this country. From what I hear, too, their lives are so austere, so bounded by prayer, they have no time to interfere in politics.

CHANCELLOR Difficulties have arisen over the ownership of the land, your majesty. The peasants say, if the land is taken away from them for building, they will starve.

HENRY Well, they don't own the land. Their livelihood isn't my worry. I want a monastery. I must have a monastery. Tell them I'll pay compensation if you

29

think it will help. Send to the Grande Chartreuse in France and ask them to send someone over to supervise. Perhaps if the local people have a monk in their midst they will be less inclined to complain. No, I'll write myself. Where's my scribe? Come here.

(Scribe moves forward)

I want to dictate a letter. 'To the abbot of the Carthusian monastery of the Grande Chartreuse. Dear Father Abbot. . . .

Music – Curtain – Fade music

READER 2　At the monastery of the Grande Chartreuse in France there was a Frenchman whose life was to be totally changed when the king's letter arrived. His name was Hugh. He himself was the son of a French soldier and had been a monk since the age of nineteen – not always in the very strict Carthusian order, but his life till this time had been dedicated to prayer and he was now forty years old. When he realized that the abbot was about to choose him for this unwelcome task of leaving a much-loved, peaceful monastery and going to a foreign country ruled by a king who was already responsible for the murder of his archbishop, he pleaded to be spared the task. But to no avail. His superior ordered him to go and, because of his vow of obedience, he had to go.

READER 1　A few years later in London Hugh was to confront the king.

Curtain

Henry seated on the throne surrounded by courtiers. Hugh stands before him. He bows

HENRY　I am delighted with the good work you are doing. When the building is complete, perhaps you would send to France for a few of your brothers to come and form the nucleus of a new community. English men and boys will need the guidance of experienced Carthusians if the community is to develop in the way we both hope.

HUGH The building will not be completed until your majesty has paid the workmen for what they have done so far.

HENRY That shall be done at once. (*Smugly*) God's work is my first concern.

HUGH (*coldly*) That's what you said last time.

HENRY How dare you? What do you mean by that?

HUGH That actions speak louder than words. Your majesty, I think we understand each other better than we used to. As your subject I offer you loyalty. As your father in God it is my duty to point out that your workmen are near starvation as they await payment; that peasants who have been forced off the land to extend the boundaries of the monastery have received no compensation and that the Lord whom we both serve said 'Inasmuch as ye did it *not* for the least of these my brethren, ye did it not for me.' Your majesty, I will not be party to this exploitation of country people.

HENRY I will see that payment is made at once.

HUGH That's what you said last time. Your majesty must settle the debt *now* – with *me*.

HENRY I haven't that amount of money available.

HUGH Then I return to France.

HENRY You *what*? You wouldn't dare.

HUGH With sorrow, I go. I can do no more here.

(*He bows and exits*)

HENRY (*raging*) Now what am I to do? Will no one rid me of this . . . (*he claps his hand to his mouth in horror*) No! No! Lord, forgive me. Quickly go and bring the prior back here.

Exit courtier

You – send for my financial advisers. He'll have to have his own way.

Curtain

READER 2 And so the monastery was completed and there Hugh established the frugal life of the Carthusians

31

	which had been his strength for so many years in France. But the peace was not to last.
READER 1	In order to increase his income the king had failed to replace bishops when they died. Then the revenue which normally supported the bishop and his household became the property of the king. Lincoln had been without a bishop for eighteen years. Several times Hugh had remonstrated with the monarch over this neglect of spiritual affairs until, unknown to him, the king gathered together ecclesiastical advisers and they decided that the prior of Witham should be the new bishop of Lincoln. As before he pleaded with his superiors to intervene to prevent his having to go. As before he was ordered to go and went.
READER 2	The people of Lincoln waited anxiously for the first sight of their new bishop.

Bells – Curtain

A crowd, the length of the stage, lining the street and craning their necks in the same direction. A buzz of talk

CITIZEN 1	Can you see anything yet?
CITIZEN 2	They can't be long now.
CITIZEN 3	Here, let this kid through to the front. He can't see a thing back here.
CITIZEN 4	Get up on my back and tell us what you can see.
CHILD	Oh quick! Quick! They're coming.
CITIZEN 1	What can you see?
CHILD	Horses – lots of them. And soldiers. Everything's shining.
CITIZEN 2	Can you see the bishop?
CHILD	Let me down. It feels as though you're going to drop me.
CITIZEN 2	Did you see the bishop?
CHILD	There are lots of priests behind the soldiers.
CITIZEN 3	What about the bishop?
CHILD	I don't know what bishops look like. I've never seen one.
CITIZEN 1	Very grand. They ride fine horses. I remember when I was confirmed the old bishop leant down

from his horse to lay his hands on my head. He was very old. I felt his hands trembling.

Enter St Hugh in mitre with crook

CITIZEN 1   My lord! (*He kneels*)

(*St Hugh pauses and smiles at the child*)

HUGH   You look surprised, my child – as well you might. Lincoln has been without a bishop for so long, you've never seen one. Come here. You see this crook? Do you know what it means?

CHILD   Dad's got a crook but his is a plain one. He's a shepherd.

HUGH   So am I. Always remember that. Whatever difficulty you find yourself in, I'm here to help you. Bless you, my child.

(*He passes on – babble of talk*)

Curtain

READER 1   St Hugh became well-known as the bishop who dismounted from his horse to confirm the children. He was a great friend of the poor and helpless and upheld their rights wherever they were being unfairly treated. There are many more stories about him, such as the tales of his pet swan who would feed from his hand and stand guard over his bed lest anyone disturb the saint while he was asleep. But we only have time to show you one more episode from his life.

READER 2   As in the days of Thomas à Becket, the king was not happy when his plans were thwarted by his clergy. The time came when the king wanted one of his own friends to be appointed Canon of Lincoln and St Hugh refused point blank, sending a message to the king to the effect that a canon should be a churchman not a courtier. The king summoned the bishop.

READER 1   To understand what happened next you need to know that Henry II was the great grandson of William the Conqueror and that William the Conqueror's mother had been one of the common people – a glove-maker from Falaise in Northern France.

Curtain

King seated on his throne surrounded by courtiers

HENRY   Remember my orders. When the bishop arrives, in no circumstances is anyone to speak to him. You are not to answer even 'Good-day'. If you like, you may even turn your backs on him. I'll cut him down to size and show him who rules here. But, before he arrives, give me a bandage. I've cut my finger.

COURTIER   Allow me, your majesty –

HENRY   No, I can do it perfectly well. Quickly. Here he comes. Now remember – not a word!

The king bows his head and busies himself sewing the bandage round his finger.

Enter Hugh. He bows

Nobody dares move. He greets the king. There is an embarrassed silence. The king continues with his needle and thread. Courtiers stand stiffly aloof. The only person at ease is Hugh. He sits down beside the king and smiles pleasantly. Not a word is said. Embarrassment deepens. Eventually, after long silence:

HUGH   (*quietly*) You remind me *so* much of your great-grandmother.

The king looks up angrily, meets his bishop's smiling eyes and his anger dissolves in laughter

HENRY   My lords! The bishop tells me I remind him of a French glovemaker.

Laughter – Curtain

READER 1   St Hugh had his way, of course.

READER 2   Years later, in his last illness, he went to Canterbury to pray at the shrine of St Thomas. While there he was summoned to a meeting in London. When he arrived he was too ill to go to the

34

meeting and took to his bed at his house in the Old Temple in Holborn. There, on 17 November in the year 1200, he died. That is why the Church honours St Hugh of Lincoln today. Now can you guess why Lincoln's Inn is so called?

Let us pray: Almighty God,
the light of the faithful
and shepherd of souls,
who set your servant Hugh to be a bishop in
    the Church,
to feed your sheep by his word
and guide them by his example:
give us grace to keep the faith which he taught
and to follow in his footsteps;
through Jesus Christ our Lord.

(ASB, Collect of a Bishop, p. 855)

Hymn: For all the saints

10. SECOND SUNDAY IN ADVENT – BIBLE SUNDAY
The Story of Mary Jones
_ *kx*

You will need:	Two Readers Mary Jones Her father Her mother Thomas Thomas, a neighbour Mr Hugh, the minister Revd Thomas Charles
Music:	Welsh male voice choir singing Welsh music

READER 1 Do you know about Captain Kidd's treasure? Captain Kidd was a pirate who lived in the seventeenth century. When he was eventually hanged in 1701 a parchment was found in his sea chest which was thought to show where he had hidden his treasure. People have been looking for it ever

35

since. In 1983 a British treasure seeker claimed to
have found some of it on a Vietnamese island but
the Vietnamese thought he was a spy and impris-
oned him. He was released on payment of a heavy
fine. On his return to this country he wasn't
prepared to say whether he would risk going back
to look again.

READER 2   What on earth has all that to do with Bible
Sunday, which the Church celebrates on the second Sunday in Advent?

READER 1   Well, we are going to tell you about a different
kind of treasure. If the story is not to seem too
simple and moralizing, you will have to use some
historical imagination and put yourself into the
place of the heroine. Her search for treasure was
very different from that of the treasure seeker in
pursuit of a pirate's wealth. The treasure she was
seeking was the opportunity to learn to read and
the opportunity to possess a book of her own.

She was only about ten years old when the story
begins. That was about two hundred years ago.
She couldn't read because there were no schools
and few people in the little Welsh valley where
she lived had ever learned. Her name was Mary
Jones.

Music – Curtain

(*Congregation seated in chapel before Mr Hugh,
the minister*)

Enter Mr and Mrs Jones and Mary

MR HUGH   Ah, here you are. Glad we are indeed to see you.
We were beginning to fear you had met with an
accident. Thomas Thomas said he'd seen you both
working at your loom this afternoon and we knew
only something serious would keep you away
from the weekday Bible class.

THOMAS   Aye, we knew you weren't ill.

MRS JONES   Mary here went over to see her gran and you
know what old people are like. She couldn't rush
away.

MARY   I'm sorry to be the cause of so much bother.

36

MR HUGH	No bother at all, my child. We rejoice that you are here safe and sound. I've good news for you too. I was in A<u>bergynolwyn</u> yesterday and heard that a travelling school is coming to the district.
MR JONES	A travelling school? Why Mary, my dear, you'll have the chance to learn to read. Your mother and I have always regretted not being able to and hoped you might one day.
MRS JONES	Then you'd be able to read the Bible to us.
MARY	Could we afford a Bible, mother?
MRS JONES	Not of our own, my dear. Books are far too expensive for the likes of us but I'm sure Mr Hugh would let you read to us out of his.
MR HUGH	Of course I would. It would give me great pleasure. I'll give you details of the school before you go. It'll only be here a few months before it moves on but, if Mary works hard, she should learn to read in that time. But we must get on now. This evening I thought we might begin to look at a letter St Paul wrote to a young man called Timothy. He wrote to him, '<u>Let no one despise your youth</u>' (1 Timothy 4.1<u>2. RS</u>V). God has plenty of work for young people to do, Mary. I wonder what he will accomplish through you, my dear? Now. . . .

Curtain – Music

READER 2	Time passed. Mary attended the school and to her great joy learnt to read well enough to be able to read the Bible for herself. Then, of course, the inevitable happened – she desperately wanted to have a Bible of her own.

Curtain

(*Jones family seated at supper*)

MARY	*Please*, father.
MR JONES	It's not that we don't *want* you to have a Bible, my dear. We just can't afford it.
MARY	Then I'll work and save up.
MRS JONES	You've no idea how expensive books are. It will take you years.

MARY	Never mind. I don't mind how long it takes.
MRS JONES	Well I'll let you have two of the hens for your own.
MARY	So I can sell their eggs? That would be marvellous. And perhaps I could grow some vegetables and take them to Abergynolwyn market?
MRS JONES	You're a good little knitter. I'll give you some wool to start you off. There's always a good market for socks.
MR JONES	And you'll need somewhere to keep your savings. I'll give you that box which used to belong to your grandfather.
MRS JONES	It'd be grand to have our own daughter to read to us from her own Bible.

Curtain – Music

READER 2	Six years passed. Mary was now well into her teens. The day came when she found that at long last she had enough money. But where did you buy books? She went to see Mr Hugh.

Curtain

MR HUGH	Yes, Mary, that is enough money for a Bible.
MARY	For a Welsh one?
MR HUGH	Yes, for a Welsh one. But I only know one man who might have a Welsh Bible for sale and that's the Reverend Thomas Charles. You know him – the man who organized the travelling school. But he lives at Bala and that's too far to go on the off-chance.
MARY	How far is it?
MR HUGH	Twenty-five miles. You can't go all that way. He doesn't get much call for Welsh Bibles and he hadn't any last time I saw him.
MARY	I'll go and ask him.
MR HUGH	But that's fifty miles there and back. A girl can't go all that way on her own. It's not safe.
MARY	God has helped me save up the money. He'll look after me on the journey.

Curtain

38

READER 1   And so she went, over the hills and along the valleys, arriving in Bala at nightfall. Mr Hugh had given her the address of a friend who would put her up for the night and the next morning she went to see Mr Charles.

Curtain

MR CHARLES   I'm sorry my dear. I only have one last copy and that has been ordered by a friend of mine. I can let you have an English one.

MARY   Oh dear. What shall I do? I can't read English very easily and I've been saving up for six years for the Welsh one. What a disappointment.

MR CHARLES   I can get you a Welsh one in a few weeks.

MARY   But I've walked twenty-five miles and I must go back today or my parents will worry themselves sick thinking something awful has happened to me.

MR CHARLES   Twenty-five *miles*? You mean fifty both ways?

MARY   Yes. It was easy enough on the way here with the excitement and hope to sustain me, but they will be long, weary miles home without either.

(*She turns to leave*)

MR CHARLES   We can't have that. Here – take it. Have the Welsh one. My friend can manage a bit longer with the English one I've lent him. I wouldn't know a moment's peace thinking I'd turned away a Christian maid empty-handed. Fifty *miles* you say? And six years saving for it? If only there were more people like you who realized what treasure lies between those covers.

MARY   Thank you, sir. Thank you very, very much and God bless you. I shall always remember your kindness.

Curtain

READER 2   So Mary left with the treasure for which she had worked so long and hard. Mary Jones is remembered to this very day because it was her determination which eventually led to the British and Foreign Bible Society being formed so that Bibles

39

should be available to people everywhere in their own languages.

READER 1   Treasure? Yes! Now listen to what Jesus says about treasure.

REST OF CLASS   Do not lay up for yourselves treasures on earth, where moth and rust consume and where thieves break in and steal, but lay up for yourselves treasure in heaven, where neither moth nor rust consumes and where thieves do not break in and steal. For where your treasure is, there will your heart be also.

(RSV, Matt. 6.19—21)

Let us pray: Blessed Lord, who hast caused all Holy Scriptures to be written for our learning: Grant that we may in such wise hear them, read, mark, learn, and inwardly digest them, that by patience, and comfort of thy holy Word, we may embrace, and ever hold fast the blessed hope of everlasting life, which thou hast given us in our Saviour Jesus Christ.

(BCP, Collect for Advent II)

Hymn: Father, hear the prayer we offer

A CHRISTMAS ASSEMBLY IN THE FORM OF A RADIO PLAY

You will need: Mary
Joseph
Rachel, the innkeeper's daughter
Innkeeper
Zebedee ⎫
Mark   ⎬ shepherds
Jonas   ⎭
Angel

Music: O little town of Bethlehem
Unto us a boy is born
O leave your sheep

40

Silent Night
'Pastorale' from Handel's *Messiah*
'Glory to God' from *Messiah*
'Andante' from Suite in G major in Handel's
Water Music

(*'O Little Town of Bethlehem'*, verse 1. *At the third line, a loud knocking is heard. Voices murmur in the background.*)

JOSEPH Mary, my dear, I'm not optimistic about this inn. It seems terribly ramshackle.

MARY That doesn't matter. I really don't feel I can go another step and we've tried everywhere else.

Pause

What a long time they're taking to answer. Do you think they heard you knocking?

JOSEPH I'll try again.

(*He knocks*)

Oh no! Now look what's happened. The knocker has come off in my hand. What a place!

MARY Try just hammering on the door.

JOSEPH I'm beginning to think that might drop off too. Oh dear – at least they wouldn't ignore us if that happened.

(*He knocks*)

(*Fade in 'O Little Town of Bethlehem'*)

RACHEL (*roughly*) Shut up, can't you? What d'you mean by coming to the front door? Get off to the kitchen to your mistress and let that be enough – ... Oh, I'm sorry, sir. Do forgive me. I thought it was young Daniel. What can have happened to him? He should be back by now. We'll never get all these people fed if he doesn't come soon.

JOSEPH You must be rushed off your feet with so many visitors in the town. But can you possibly find room for just two more?

RACHEL Oh no, sir. I'm very sorry. We've crammed in more than the authorities would allow as it is. But what can they expect at census time? No sir, we

41

	can't help you. Lots of people are having to sleep rough, you know.
JOSEPH	Yes, I do know. We've passed many along the road. But we're in special difficulty. My wife's baby is due and will probably be born quite soon and she *must* have somewhere to rest. *Please*, isn't there anywhere we could go?
MARY	Please . . . it's so cold out here. It frightens me to think what will happen to my baby if it is born out here on a night like this.
RACHEL	Oh, you poor dear. What can we do? There really isn't anywhere to go at all unless . . .
INNKEEPER	(*loudly interrupting*) Come in or go out, but keep that door shut. Rachel, you're wanted in the kitchen. What's going on here?
RACHEL	I was just telling this gentleman we were full, but they're in real trouble and I wondered if they could go out in the stable?
INNKEEPER	Well, I haven't had time to clean it out and it'll probably stink to high heaven, but you can show them where it is if you like.
MARY	That *is* kind of you. (*Pause*) What a story this will be to tell my son of the night when he was born. We shall always remember your kindness.
INNKEEPER	Son, eh? Supposing it's a girl? Oh cheer up, sir, I was only joking. Anyway, my daughter's a great help to me. Worth their weight in gold in the hotel trade, girls are. What's your line of business?
JOSEPH	I'm a carpenter.
INNKEEPER	Help the lady, Rachel. Come and have a drink, sir. You'll need it before the night's over and none of the servants will want to come down to the stable at this hour of the night.
JOSEPH	It's kind of you, but I'd feel happier to see my wife settled.
INNKEEPER	As you please. When you've had as many kids as I have, you won't take much notice. Well, good luck to you. Hope it's a boy!
JOSEPH	(*thoughtfully to himself*) A boy? Yes. There's no doubt it will be a boy.

(Fade in '*Unto us a boy is born*')

42

ALL   Unto us a boy is born
King of all creation
Came into a world forlorn
The lord of every na-a-a-a-tion.

Cradled in a stall was he
With sleepy cows and asses
But the very beast could see
That he all men surpa-a-a-a-ses.

(Fade in 'Pastorale' from Handel's *Messiah*)

ZEBEDEE   95 – 96 – 97 – 98 – 99! One missing! On a night like this too! It'll just have to take care of itself.

MARK   Come off it, lad! Call yourself a shepherd? You youngsters have no idea. You can't leave a sheep lost on the hillside at the mercy of wolves, whatever the weather. I'll come and help you if Jonas here will keep an eye on my flock while we're gone.

JONAS   Well, don't be long. This flock is too big for just one person to look after, especially at lambing time.

ZEBEDEE   Thanks for the offer, Mark, but you stay with Jonas. I didn't really mean I'd leave it wandering. It shouldn't take long to find it in this light. Seems much brighter than usual tonight.

JONAS   It's that star up there. I've never noticed it before, but it seems to be getting brighter and brighter.

ZEBEDEE   Well, I'll be off.

MARK   Wait a moment, lad – Look! What's that in the sky?

ZEBEDEE   The light's getting brighter and brighter.

(Fade in 'Glory to God' from *Messiah*)

JONAS   (*terrified*) it's coming towards us – Run! – Hide!

ANGEL   'Fear not: for, behold, I bring you good tidings of great joy, which shall be to all people. For unto you is born this day in the city of David, a Saviour, which is Christ the Lord. And this shall be a sign unto you: you shall find the baby wrapped in swaddling clothes, lying in a manger.'

(AV, Luke 2.10–12)

43

(Finish 'Glory to God')

Pause

MARK   Are you still there, lad?

ZEBEDEE   What was it, Mark?

JONAS   The light was blinding. I'm shaking. Did you hear anything too?

ZEBEDEE   Mark – *What was it?*

MARK   It must have been a messenger from God. The light seemed to burn right into me and I've never felt so terrified.

ZEBEDEE   Me too. It made me ashamed of all that silly talk of leaving the lost sheep to take care of itself. Just for the moment I felt like a lost sheep myself. I wonder what the voice meant about a Saviour which is Christ the Lord?

MARK   Don't bother your head with things beyond it. Anyway, you're in luck. There's your lost sheep over there. It must have been frightened by the light, or else it saw its way back by it. It'll come if you call it now.

ZEBEDEE   It'll come, yes, and I know what I'll do with it. If a Saviour has really been born in Bethlehem, then I'm going to see, and the sheep would be a good present for him.

MARK   Hurry up, then. I don't want to stay away from the flock too long tonight. They're a bit restless after what has happened.

ZEBEDEE   Just wait while I get my cloak.

ALL   O leave your sheep, your lambs that follow after,
O leave the brook, the pasture and the crook;
No longer weep, turn weeping into laughter,
O shepherds seek your goal,
Your Lord, your Lord, who cometh to console,
Your Lord, your Lord, who cometh to console.

(Fade in 'Water Music')

ZEBEDEE   This can't be the place. The Saviour wouldn't be born in a stable.

MARK   Well, the angel said we should find him lying in a manger, so it's worth having a look. Something must be going on in there. There's so much light again.

ZEBEDEE It's a scandal – all these people – nowhere for them to go –

MARK Sh – sh – ! Be quiet, can't you? I want to have a peep through here before we go in.

Pause

Oh-h-h!

Music

ZEBEDEE Let me see. What is it?

MARK The stable is full of the most beautiful light and there *is* a child lying in the manger. The light seems to be playing round his head. Oh Zebedee – something wonderful has happened. I don't understand, but it's *good* to be here. Don't talk. I *must* go in, scruffy as I am. Did you ever know such peace? I think truly this must be the Son of God.

ALL Silent night, holy night,
Starry skies beaming bright –
Guard the Virgin mother mild –
Watching o'er the Holy Child –
Sleep in heav'nly peace
Sleep in heav'nly peace.

Silent night, holy night,
Shepherds lone hail the light.
Hark, the wondrous angel throng,
Hail the morn with joyful song:
Christ the Saviour is born,
Christ the Saviour is born.

SPRING TERM

EPIPHANY – 6 January

You will need an elaborately gift-wrapped package.

It is not all that often that we are back at school in time for Epiphany. In fact most of us probably feel rather hard done by when this happens. Cheer up! It must mean that Easter is early this year and the holidays aren't as far away as we think. Otherwise there is no sense in being back at school on the twelfth day of Christmas. We should still be celebrating!

Do you remember all those things my true love gave to me on the twelfth day of Christmas? Each year *The Times* works out the cost of all those gifts – so much an hour for pipers piping and drummers drumming, the cost of seven swans (always supposing you can buy them), six geese, so much for gold rings, French hens, right down to the cost of the partridge and a pear tree bought from the local nursery. It's a lighthearted seasonal tilt at the rate of inflation which so dogs our footsteps throughout the rest of the year. The total cost, of course, runs into thousands of pounds and it rises as the years go by.

Working out the cost of a gift is also perhaps a gentle criticism of the way in which Christmas has become commercialized. Think for a moment about your own Christmas. Try to be honest with yourself. What was best about it? Maybe you will think of the present that gave you most pleasure. What was it? Why did it give you so much pleasure? Was it something you had really wanted for a long time? Were you pleased just because someone had spent a lot of money on you? – or was it because it was a sign that they loved you? Maybe your best moment was seeing the pleasure on someone else's face when they unwrapped the present you had given them. Had you spent a lot of money on it? – or a lot of loving thought? Did your pleasure come from seeing people you don't often see? – family gatherings? parties? Maybe your greatest pleasure was the food and drink of the season. Or was it just something about the Christmas atmosphere?

Do you remember Dickens trying to put this into words? He is

46

describing Scrooge accompanying the Ghost of Christmas Present and seeing the poor people coming out to take their dinners to the bakers' shops to be cooked.

The sight of these poor revellers appeared to interest the Spirit very much, for he stood with Scrooge beside him in a baker's doorway, and taking off the covers as their bearers passed, sprinkled incense on their dinners from his torch. And it was a very uncommon kind of torch, for once or twice when there were angry words between some dinner-carriers who had jostled with each other, he shed a few drops of water on them from it, and their good humour was restored directly. For they said, it was a shame to quarrel upon Christmas Day. And so it was! God love it, so it was!

(*A Christmas Carol*, Charles Dickens, Stave 1)

What happens to this spirit during the rest of the year? Where does the love go that we express so warmly in the giving of presents at this season? Although it's nearly a fortnight since we exchanged gifts, the Church is today remembering the great gift-giving which accompanied the arrival of the wise men from the East. Do you remember what happened?

When they saw the star, they rejoiced with exceeding great joy. And when they were come into the house, they saw the young child with Mary his mother, and fell down, and worshipped him: and when they had opened their treasures, they presented unto him gifts: gold, and frankincense, and myrrh.

(AV, Matthew 2.10–11)

There's something mysterious about those gifts. We are taught that gold represented the kingship of Christ, frankincense his priesthood, and myrrh his suffering and death. Strange gifts to offer a small child. Did it really happen just like that? More recently scholars have suggested that these were the tools of the trade of magicians and that they were laying them at the feet of the Christ child – giving them up, turning to a new life in him. And yet they too had to go back to the old routine, just as we are here today taking up the routine of school life. Had meeting the Christ child made any difference to them? T. S. Eliot had no doubt that it had changed them. Do you remember how, in *Journey of the Magi* he makes one of them say

'We returned to our places, these Kingdoms,
But no longer at ease here, in the old dispensation,
With an alien people clutching their gods.'

(*Journey of the Magi*, 11.40–42)

47

So what about us? You see Epiphany isn't just about the gifts the wise men brought to Jesus. Nor is it just about all those things my true love gave to me on the twelfth day of Christmas. The word Epiphany means 'manifesting' – 'showing'. Jesus was shown to the wise men. They recognized him as God and so were changed. He gave them the greatest gift of all – himself. He offers that same gift to us – gift-wrapped in all the happiness of the season.

(*indicate the package*)

Are we going to open the gift he offers us? – get to know him? Or are we just going to enjoy the wrappings and put the pretty parcel away unopened with the fairy from the top of the Christmas tree so that we can use the wrappings again next year? The gift is here – ours for the opening – but the choice of whether to open it or not is ours.

Let us pray: On this day, Lord God,
by a guiding star you revealed your
    Only-begotten Son
to all the peoples of the world.
Lead us from the faith by which we know you
    now
to the vision of your glory, face to face.
We make our prayer through our Lord.

(*Divine Office, Roman Rite*,
concluding prayer for Epiphany p. 319)

12. ACCESSION OF QUEEN ELIZABETH II
6 February

You will need: Readers
Saul
Servant
Variable number of girls (one speaking part)
Samuel
Crowd
Jesse
Variable number of leaders of Bethlehem (one speaking)

48

Seven sons of Jesse
David
Nathan
Bathsheba
Serving girl

Music: Handel's *Zadok the Priest* (essential)
Vaughan Williams' *Fantasia on a Theme of Thomas Tallis* (or equivalent)

READER Today is the anniversary of the accession of our Queen in 1952. It is the day on which her father died and she became queen not only of this country but of the whole Commonwealth. For her it must be a day of sad memories. Her father had been ill and the young Princess Elizabeth with her husband, the Duke of Edinburgh, had set off on a tour of the Commonwealth which had originally been planned for the King himself, but he was not well enough to undertake it.

They had flown to Kenya on 1 February and, after fulfilling various public engagements, had gone to spend the night of 5 February at the famous Treetops Hotel. This hotel is built in a large tree in a forest and overlooks a water hole so that visitors are able to observe the wild animals coming to drink.

That night King George VI died and the news was broken to the new queen the following afternoon by the Duke of Edinburgh. She and the duke at once flew home to London to be greeted at the airport by the nation's leaders. It was a time of sadness for everyone. George VI had been a much-loved king and the nation mourned his death and grieved with the young princess now embarking on the onerous role of monarch. Most of her life had been spent preparing for this moment but nobody had expected it to come so soon. People were confident that she would be a good queen and the time was hailed as the dawn of a new Elizabethan age. You might like to think about that later. What have we as a nation achieved during her reign? But remember, our

49

shortcomings are not her fault and she herself sets us a fine example of service so that we can rejoice at the anniversary of the day she came to the throne.

To celebrate the occasion we are going to show you three brief scenes of the choosing of the first three kings of Israel. First, Saul.

Enter in front of curtain Saul and a servant

SAUL   Don't keep on about the donkeys. I'm sick to death of the donkeys. Who let them out, anyway? We've been looking for them for days. I'm sure father didn't mean us to come this far when he sent us out to search.

SERVANT   But master –

SAUL   No more 'Buts'. If we don't turn back now, father will stop worrying about his precious donkeys and start worrying about us.

SERVANT   Forgive me, master. I was only going to say that there's a man living in this town who has the reputation for knowing all sorts of things. People come to consult him from miles around. He might be able to tell us where they are.

SAUL   What use is that to us? We've nothing on us we can give him, so we can hardly go and ask for his help.

SERVANT   I've a small silver coin which I keep for emergencies. We could give him that.

Enter from opposite direction girls carrying water jars

SERVANT   Excuse me, ladies. Can you tell us where to find the seer?

GIRL 1   Yes, indeed. He's just ahead of you. If you hurry, you'll catch up with him. He has come to bless the sacrifice to be made on the hill over there.

SERVANT   Thank you. Master, let's try, just this once more.

SAUL   Very well.

Curtain

Samuel standing centre surrounding by respectful crowd. Saul approaches

50

SAUL   Excuse me, sir. Can you tell me where the seer lives?

SAMUEL   I am the seer. Go on up the hill and join us in the worship and then come and dine with me tonight. The donkeys you've been looking for are quite safe but the Lord has sent you to me for a special purpose.

SAUL   How did you know we were looking for donkeys? What do you mean that the Lord has a special purpose for me? I belong to the smallest tribe in Israel and my family has no status.

SAMUEL   The Lord has spoken to me about you. Come with us now to the sacrifice and the feast and I will tell you more in the morning.

Exeunt – Curtain – Music

Enter in front of curtain Samuel, Saul and the servant

SAUL   Thank you again for all your help. I'm most grateful.

SAMUEL   Send your servant on ahead. There is one more thing I have to tell you before you go.

Saul waves servant ahead and he leaves

SAMUEL   Saul, what I have to tell is of the utmost importance. The Lord has chosen you to be the first king of his people Israel and has appointed me to anoint you with oil as the sign of his favour. He will be with you as you strive to do his will. Come with me and I will anoint you.

Exeunt. Music

READER   Samuel took a jar of oil and poured some of it on Saul's head and from that time onward Saul was aware of his destiny, although it was not until some time later that he was actually crowned and acclaimed king by the people.

Time passed and Saul became self-centred, more concerned with his own importance than God's will. Again God spoke to Samuel, this time telling him to go to Bethlehem to anoint one of

51

the sons of Jesse as the future king. Samuel feared Saul's anger but was told to go and offer a sacrifice and to trust God.

Enter Samuel in front of curtain to be met by Jesse and the leaders of Bethlehem

LEADER 1   We are honoured by your visit, sir, but we are troubled as to the reason for it. Do you come in peace or do you come to rebuke us?

SAMUEL   I have come to offer a sacrifice to the Lord and would stay at the house of Jesse.

JESSE   You are welcome indeed, sir.

SAMUEL   And I should like to meet your sons. The Lord has chosen one of them to do him a special service.

JESSE   An honour indeed. Come into the house.

Curtain

Here are three of my sons.

SAMUEL   Eliab – (*aside*) How handsome he is – I rejoice to meet you. (*aside*) But he is not the one.
Abinidab – (*aside*) – No. He is not the one.
Shammah – (*aside*) Nor is this the one, strong though he seems.

Music as seven sons pass before Samuel to be greeted warmly in turn but rejected with a sad shake of Samuel's head. Fade music

Have you any more sons?

JESSE   Only the youngest. He is out in the fields looking after the sheep.

SAMUEL   Call him too.

Music while they wait, the other sons standing around talking quietly to each other

Enter David

DAVID   My name is David, sir. You wished to see me?

SAMUEL   The Lord has chosen you to be the next king of his people.

DAVID   King? Me? But I am a shepherd.

SAMUEL   You shall be the shepherd king of his people. Kneel, David. The Lord has commanded me to anoint you.

52

Curtain. Music (Introduction to *Zadok the Priest*)

READER   Many years later David's son, Solomon, was to become king. By that time Samuel was dead and his place had been taken by Nathan, the prophet. A power struggle had developed as King David lay dying and one of Solomon's half brothers had had himself crowned king. Nathan approached Solomon's mother.

Enter Nathan and Bathsheba in front of curtain. Continue music faintly

NATHAN   Your majesty, have you not heard that Adonijah has had himself crowned king? I'm sure his majesty knows nothing about it. Would you approach him and tell him? Otherwise I fear for your safety and the safety of your son Solomon. If you go first, I'll follow at once to confirm what you have said.

BATHSHEBA   Let us go without delay.

Exit Nathan. Curtain. David in bed attended by a serving girl. Continue music quietly

BATHSHEBA   My lord, you made me a solemn promise that Solomon would succeed you as king. But Adonijah has made himself king. Is that what you really intended?

Enter Nathan

NATHAN   Your majesty, have you given any authority to Adonijah to succeed you as king? There are crowds feasting and shouting 'Long live King Adonijah!' Is this your majesty's will?

BATHSHEBA   Tell us what you want, my lord, and it shall be done.

DAVID   'Take my court officials with you; let my son Solomon ride my own mule, and escort him down to the spring of Gihon, where Zadok and Nathan are to anoint him as king of Israel. Then blow the trumpet and shout 'Long live King Solomon!'

(GNB, I Kings 1.33–34)

Curtain slowly – Music to coincide with the words
'Zadok the Priest' and 'Nathan the prophet'. Con-
tinue music ad lib

READER And that great anthem by Handel is sung at the coronation of our own kings and queens. The words themselves have been used in coronation services since the coronation of King Edgar the Peaceful at Bath in 973.

Our own queen was anointed just like those Old Testament kings as a sign of God's grace being given to her. Many of you will have seen the ampulla in the form of an eagle, which holds the oil, and the spoon into which the oil is poured. Both are among the crown jewels in the Tower of London. The Archbishop of Canterbury dipped his thumb into the oil and anointed her 'with holy oil, as kings, priests and prophets were anointed' thus making her queen in God's sight.

On the evening of her coronation, the queen spoke to her people. She said,

'When I spoke to you last, at Christmas, I asked you all, whatever your religion, to pray for me on the day of my Coronation – to pray that God would give me wisdom and strength to carry out the promises that I should then be making.'
(*Times Coronation supplement*, June 1953)

As we celebrate her reign of over a quarter of a century, let us join together in singing our national anthem, using it as our prayer for her today.

13. BEING ALONE

Today and tomorrow, I'd like us to think about being alone. *Not* being lonely. There is a difference, if you stop to think.

If I say the word 'lonely', the chances are you'll conjure up in your mind's eye a picture of an old lady, muffled in cardigans, shut up in the house which has been her home for fifty years or more. The paint is peeling, nobody visits her or troubles about her until one day the milkman wonders why she hasn't taken in the milk. The police are called to open up the house and she is found at the foot of the stairs with bones broken after a nasty fall.

You know the kind of thing. We all know it happens. But I wouldn't presume to tell you anything about it. Because the majority of your generation set a shining example to the majority of my generation in the love and care which you show for the elderly.

But what about being *alone*? Is it necessarily an unhappy state? I'm sure there are times when you all stump off to your rooms and probably slam the door. This is right and proper – not the door-slamming bit, but the need to get away from people and just be still.

The hint I would like to drop you is that adults feel the same way. Matthew Arnold wrote a beautiful poem about a woman who didn't find this peace until death:

Strew on her roses, roses
And never a spray of yew
In quiet she reposes;
Ah, would that I did too!

Her mirth the world required;
She bathed it in smiles of glee.
But her heart was tired, tired,
And now they let her be.

Her life was turning, turning,
In mazes of heat and sound.
But for peace her soul was yearning,
And now peace laps her round.

(Requiescat)

It really shouldn't be necessary to wait for death to bring peace. But we do have to be sensitive to each other's need for quiet. One of the best accounts I know of this sensitivity to another person's need to withdraw from the hurly-burly comes in *Cider with Rosie*.

For those of you who haven't yet read it, it is the true story of a childhood spent in a tiny Cotswold village about fifty years ago. Young Laurie Lee's mother is quite scatterbrained. She's an ebullient, lovable character, quite overwhelmed by the impossible task of rearing her large family with no father and no income. Yet somehow, when she is there, they are all happy. As a housewife she's a disaster; as a mother she succeeds because she is so full of love. And something of this love rubs off on her young son Laurie, because he even senses his mother's very real need to be quiet and to unwind.

'I would lie awake in my still-light bedroom and hear the chime of the piano below, a ragged chord, a poignant pause, then a twinkling wagtail run. Brash yet melancholy, coarse yet wistful, it would rise in a jangling burst, then break and shiver as soft as water and lap round my listening head. She would play some waltzes and sometimes I would hear her singing – a cool lone voice, uncertainly rising, addressed to her own reflection. They were sounds of peace, half-edged with sleep, yet disturbing, almost shamefully moving. I wanted to run to her then, and embrace her as she played. But somehow I never did.'

(Cider with Rosie)

Jesus had the same problem. During his ministry there were constant demands on his compassion. Crowds pressed in on all sides begging him to heal them. He never refused. He gave of himself constantly and so he too had this very great need to withdraw and renew his strength. And even his closest friends didn't understand. After one particularly gruelling evening of renewing life and hope in the sick, we are told Jesus got up early in the morning to go away alone to pray. And what happened? Dear Peter, that overwhelming, enthusiastic, lovable man, who always managed to say the wrong thing and do the wrong thing, who almost always spoke first and thought afterwards, rushed off after him – Oh master, master, everyone's looking for you. You're a huge success. Come on back and do some more.

See how easily it's done? That precious moment of stillness destroyed. Let's do our best to recognize when people want to be alone and need to be alone.

Let us pray: Lord, you said to your disciples, 'Peace I leave with you, my peace I give unto you,' Grant such times of quietness to each one of us that we may truly know in our own hearts that peace which the world cannot give.

Hymn: Dear Lord and Father of mankind

14. BEING ALONE IN A CROWD

Yesterday we thought about our need to be alone sometimes. Today I want to think about a different aspect of being alone – being alone in a crowd.

For some of you it's a fairly recent experience. That long walk up the drive on your first day is still fairly fresh in your minds. I'm sure I'm safe in saying that you thought everybody had a friend except you. Then you found yourself in a class full of strange faces. How on earth am I going to make friends, you thought. But you did – quite successfully – because on that occasion you didn't assume that everyone was against you.

But being alone in a crowd can be an awful experience because, if we once lose the capacity to see the crowd as a lot of separate individuals just as self-conscious as we are, we start growing a shell to pretend that we don't really mind being alone, and that shell makes it much harder for other people to get to know us.

Here's another poem by Matthew Arnold. He is usually regarded as a rather daunting Victorian gentleman, a school inspector, solemn and rather humourless. This view probably derives more from his rather solemn, bewhiskered countenance than from actual fact. There is a delightful story of Max Beerbohm idly removing the side-whiskers from Arnold's photograph and being amazed by the sympathetic, fun-loving face then revealed. Be that as it may, there is a sad story about young Matthew Arnold. On holiday in Switzerland he met a beautiful girl, 'Marguerite', and fell in love with her. She was rather a flirt, didn't understand how serious this rather solemn Englishman was, possibly led him on and then jilted him. He was shattered. Out of this experience came this poem. He speaks of individuals as islands in a vast sea and says surely we weren't meant to be like this? Surely we are intended to be part of a great continent, all joined together in love and understanding of each other.

Yes! in the sea of life enisled,
With echoing straits between us thrown,
Dotting the shoreless watery wild,
We mortal millions live *alone*.
The islands feel the enclasping flow,
And then their endless bounds they know.

But when the moon their hollows lights
And they are swept by balms of spring,

57

And in their glens, on starry nights,
The nightingales divinely sing;
And lovely notes, from shore to shore,
Across the sounds and channels pour –

Oh! then a longing like despair
Is to their farthest caverns sent;
For surely once, they feel, we were
Parts of a single continent!
Now round us spreads the watery plain –
Oh might our marges meet again!

Who order'd that their longing's fire
Should be, as soon as kindled, cool'd?
Who renders vain their deep desire? –
A God, a God their severance ruled!
And bade betwixt their shores to be
The unplumb'd, salt, estranging sea.

We all have a need for each other. We aren't islands, self-sufficient
and alone.

Do you remember the story of Jesus healing the woman with a
haemorrhage? For the disciples she was one of the crowd, but her
heart went out and her hand went out too to touch Jesus, and he
recognized her as a *person* with her own needs and longings. Listen to
the story in St Mark's version.

There was a woman who had suffered terribly from severe bleeding
for twelve years, even though she had been treated by many doctors.
She had spent all her money, but instead of getting better she got
worse all the time. (Do you remember how St Luke, the doctor, left
that bit out about the medical treatment having made her worse?)
She had heard about Jesus, so she came in the crowd behind him,
saying to herself, 'If I just touch his clothes, I will get well'. She
touched his cloak, and her bleeding stopped at once; and she had the
feeling inside herself that she was healed of her trouble. At once Jesus
knew that power had gone out of him, so he turned round in the
crowd and asked, 'Who touched my clothes?' His disciples answered,
'You see how the people are crowding you; why do you ask who
touched you?' But Jesus kept looking round to see who had done it.
The woman realized what had happened to her, so she came trembling with fear, knelt at his feet, and told him the whole truth. Jesus said

to her, 'My daughter, your faith has made you well. Go in peace, and be healed of your trouble.'

(GNB, Mark 5.25–34)

What has this to do with our being alone in a crowd? Just this – that in the world today WE are Jesus' eyes and arms and heart to see and help and love each other. If there is anyone in this school who feels alone, it is the fault of each one of us. And listen to the judgement that is upon us – for me these are the most frightening verses in the Bible.

'Away from me, you that are under God's curse! . . . I was hungry but you would not feed me, thirsty but you would not give me a drink; I was a stranger but you would not welcome me in your homes, naked but you would not clothe me; I was sick and in prison but you would not take care of me.' Then they will answer him, 'When, Lord, did we ever see you hungry or thirsty or a stranger or naked or sick or in prison, and would not help you?' The King will reply, 'I tell you, whenever you refused to help one of these least important ones, you refused to help me.'

(GNB, Matt. 25.41–45)

That doesn't necessarily mean some poor old lady living on her own, although it might do; it might be the person sitting next to you in class who has just fallen out with her best friend, or who has never had a best friend. Let's make sure we don't have anyone who is or feels an island on her own in this school.

Let us pray:　O Lord,
teach us our need of one another;
make us remember how much we owe to one
　　another;
and fill us with a desire to help one another
for Jesus Christ's sake.

Hymn: Help us to help each other, Lord

15. LOURDES – 11 February
The Story of St Bernadette

You will need: Two Readers
Bernadette Soubirous
Toinette, her sister
Jeanne Abadie (Baloume), a friend
Mme Soubirous
M. Leon-Jacques-Vital Dutour, Imperial pro-
curator
Père Peyramale, curé of Lourdes
Two Aunts
Variable number of girls – seven speaking parts

Music: The Lourdes hymn which may be played on the
piano.
A bell for the Angelus

READER 1   Most of you will have heard of Lourdes. Those of
you who are Roman Catholics will probably have
been reminded that today the Church is celebrating the visions of Our Lady of Lourdes granted
there to a poor peasant girl, Bernadette Soubirous. It all happened a little over a hundred years
ago in 1858 and caused this small town in the
Pyrenees to become perhaps the best-known
place of pilgrimage in Europe today.

READER 2   Each year close on three million pilgrims visit
Lourdes. Reactions vary from the joy and thankfulness of those who find healing there to critic-
isms of commercialization from others of a different turn of mind. The only way to form your own
opinion is to go there yourself. Perhaps one day
you will.

READER 1   Come with us now to Lourdes, back in time to 11
February 1858. There we find a family living in
acute poverty. The father is out of work. He had
once been a miller but the business has failed and
the family are close to starvation. His eldest
daughter, Bernadette, who is fourteen, is out
gathering wood with her sister and a friend.

60

Curtain

BERNADETTE	Come on, Toinette. We haven't anything like enough yet.
BALOUME	I've found some bones. We should get a few centimes for them.
TOINETTE	Race you across the stream.
BALOUME	All right. It'll warm us up.
BERNADETTE	You know I can't. It'll bring on my asthma.
TOINETTE	Spoilsport. Come on, Baloume.

Exeunt

BERNADETTE   Wait for me!

(*She sits down and starts to remove her shoes and stockings.*)

The Angelus rings (3 strokes – pause – 3 strokes – pause – 3 strokes – pause – 9 strokes)

(*Bernadette listens – stands – makes the sign of the cross*)

Curtain

READER 2   A deep and frightening stillness came over the place. Bernadette looked up and saw a lady wearing a white dress and a blue sash with a yellow rose on each foot which matched the colour of the rosary she was holding. She rubbed her eyes and fumbled in her pocket to find her rosary. She tried to make the sign of the cross but her arm would not move. The vision made the sign of the cross and slowly Bernadette copied her. She began to say her rosary and, as she did so, the lady of the vision allowed the beads of her own rosary to slide through her fingers although her own lips did not move. When Bernadette had finished, the lady vanished.

(*Lourdes hymn quietly*)

Curtain

(*Bernadette putting on her shoes and socks*)

Enter Toinette and Baloume

61

BERNADETTE	(*thoughtfully*) I wish you hadn't run off. Something has happened that I don't understand. Did you see anything?
BALOUME	Yes, you on your knees saying your prayers.
TOINETTE	Daft I call it. We didn't come out here to pray. There's work to be done if we aren't all to freeze tonight. Look how much wood I've got and you haven't got a thing yet. And it's freezing cold. Come on, Bernadette. Wake up.
BALOUME	What's up? You look as if you've seen a ghost.
BERNADETTE	I've seen someone. I don't know who. If you promise not to tell, I'll tell you.
TOINETTE AND BALOUME	(*solemnly*) We promise.
BERNADETTE	Well, it was like this. . . .

Curtain

(*Lourdes hymn*)

READER 1	Of course the girls didn't keep their promise and gradually the story got around the town.
READER 2	Three days later on the Sunday Bernadette, accompanied this time by ten young girls, set out once again for the grotto.

(*Enter Bernadette in front of curtain accompanied by a string of girls*)

GIRL 1	Which grotto?
GIRL 2	You don't mean the old rubbish dump?
GIRL 3	Well, I've brought some holy water to throw at it if you see it again. The devil can't stand holy water and my father says you're seeing the devil.
GIRL 4	The devil doesn't have yellow roses on his feet.
GIRL 3	My father says the devil can take any form.

(*Exit Bernadette ahead of the others*)

GIRL 5	My mother would kill me if she knew I'd come.
GIRL 6	Aren't you frightened, Bernadette? Oh, where's she gone?
GIRL 7	She must have gone on ahead – come on! We shall be missing it.

(*Exeunt, chattering – Lourdes hymn*)

Curtain

READER 1	The girls found Bernadette kneeling in ecstasy. They were unable to bring her to her senses and had to fetch some adults to carry her. Her mother forbade her to return to the grotto, but it was an order Bernadette could not possibly keep.
READER 2	Eighteen times the lady appeared to her. On the ninth occasion she was told 'Go and drink at the spring and wash in it'. That was just a fortnight after the first appearance. Later that same evening she was summoned with her father to the office of the Imperial Procurator.

Curtain

(Procurator seated)

PROCURATOR	Come in, Mme Soubirous. I'm glad you've come with your daughter. Sit down, won't you?
BERNADETTE	We shall make your chairs dirty.
PROCURATOR	As you will, but I've a lot of questions and you will get tired.

(Bernadette sits cross-legged on the floor)

	That's better. Now, tell me – this lady of yours. It's a fortnight since you first saw her, I believe?
BERNADETTE	That's correct.
PROCURATOR	And she told you to tell no one you had seen her?
BERNADETTE	No. She didn't speak at all on the first two occasions. The third time Madame Milhet had asked me to ask her to write down her name.
PROCURATOR	And what did she reply?
BERNADETTE	'That isn't necessary.' Then she asked me to visit her for a fortnight and said 'I don't promise to make you happy in this world, but in the next.'
PROCURATOR	So the lady did not belong to this world?
BERNADETTE	How can I tell?
PROCURATOR	What did she look like?
BERNADETTE	Very beautiful. I've told you before. Young too.
PROCURATOR	How many times have you see her?
BERNADETTE	Nine so far.
PROCURATOR	And has she ever spoken to you again?
BERNADETTE	Yes. The day before yesterday.

PROCURATOR	What did she say then?
BERNADETTE	I cannot tell you. The lady said 'I forbid you to repeat this to anyone'.
PROCURATOR	To *anyone*? What about your confessor?
BERNADETTE	No. Not even to him.
PROCURATOR	Did she not say anything you can repeat?
BERNADETTE	When I saw her yesterday she said 'Penitence . . . Penitence . . . You're to pray to God for sinners' –
PROCURATOR	Go on.
BERNADETTE	Then today she said 'Go and drink at the spring and wash in it'.
PROCURATOR	What spring?
MME SOUBIROUS	That's the trouble, sir. There isn't a spring there. There were about three hundred people watching her. She didn't seem to be in a trance all the time but was obviously looking for water. Whenever she headed for the river something – or someone – called her back. Eventually she started scrabbling in the mud and put some in her mouth and smeared it on her face. It was eerie to watch.
PROCURATOR	Has the doctor seen her?
MME SOUBIROUS	We can't afford doctors, sir.
PROCURATOR	Has it occurred to you that your daughter might be mad? She must see a doctor and she is not to visit the grotto again.

Curtain – Lourdes hymn

READER 1	It was impossible for Bernadette to obey an order like that. She returned to the grotto and water began to flow from the spring she had discovered. Now you know how springs of water are always associated with appearances of Mary, the mother of Jesus. The appearance of water brought about a change in the attitude of people to the grotto. They began to regard it as a holy place in its own right.
READER 2	Then, on 2 March, nearly three weeks after the first vision, Bernadette's lady spoke again. 'Go and tell the priests that people are to come here in procession.' So Bernadette set off to tell the parish priest.

Enter in front of curtain Bernadette and two aunts

AUNT 1	What will you say?
BERNADETTE	I'm not sure yet. You will hear.
AUNT 2	He's got an awful temper. Aren't you scared?
BERNADETTE	Yes, but I must do what my lady says.

(*They cross stage and knock on door. Door opened by the curé himself*)

BERNADETTE Monsieur, you must have heard of the lady who has spoken to me at the grotto. Today she has given me a message for you. She said 'Go and tell the priests that people are to come here in procession.'

PEYRAMALE How dare you come bothering me with your mad talk? What nonsense is this? Processions indeed! Be gone!

(*He shoos them fiercely away back across the stage and returns to his house slamming the door*)

(*Lourdes hymn*)

(*The women return, fearfully, and Bernadette again knocks*)

PEYRAMALE What, you again?

BERNADETTE Monsieur, I must repeat the message of my lady. She really did say 'Go and tell the priests that people are to come here in procession'.

(*Peyramale raises his arms in fury and the women scuttle away*)

(*Lourdes hymn*)

(*The third time Bernadette slowly returns alone. She knocks. He opens the door*)

BERNADETTE (*with great dignity she drops a curtsy*) Monsieur, I forgot to say that the lady also told me to tell the priests to have a chapel built there.

PEYRAMALE But my dear girl, you can't go building chapels and having processions if you don't know who you are supposed to be honouring. Who *is* this lady?

BERNADETTE I don't know her name.

PEYRAMALE Well, you'd better go and find out. (*He retreats indoors*)

Exit Bernadette

READER 1   Three weeks later, on Lady Day, Bernadette went to the grotto very early in the morning. Again she prayed in the presence of her beautiful lady and, when she had finished, asked most politely if she would tell her who she was. Four times she repeated the question and eventually received the reply, 'I am the Immaculate Conception' – *not* 'I am Our Lady of Lourdes' or 'St Mary the Virgin' – but something abstract. Here is a mystery to ponder.

READER 2   Bernadette saw her beautiful lady twice more. Eventually the parish priest arranged for her to become a boarder in the local convent school. She was not very bright and her education was suffering still more through all the publicity. At the age of twenty-one she decided to join the community as a novice.

READER 1   Two years later the Basilica of the Immaculate Conception had been built and Bernadette attended the first Mass. Later that year she was sent to the mother house of her community many miles away where she spent the rest of her life, never again returning to her birthplace. She sought no publicity for herself and years later when asked if she was sad that the days when she had been granted her vision were over she replied,

READER 2   No. I was like a broom. When the sweeping is finished, you put it behind the door and forget about it.

Let us pray: Almighty God,
who chose the weak to confound the strong,
and whose only Son, Our Lord Jesus Christ,
thanked you that you had revealed to babes
things which you had hidden from the wise
    and prudent,
keep us from glorying in our own importance,
from wanting to be noticed, praised,
    honoured, preferred before others,

66

and grant that we may grow in humility
as we learn to serve you in one another.

Hymn: Father, hear the prayer we offer

16. ST POLYCARP – 23 February

I want you this morning to think of the very oldest man you know.
How many of you are picturing someone of over 80? Over 90? What
is he like? Can he still get about on his own? Does he have someone
to look after him? Is his memory failing? Does he walk with a stick? Is
he kind – or is he crotchety? Life may have done a lot to sadden us by
the time we are 80 plus. But sometimes we are privileged to meet an
elderly person with a tremendous zest for life who nevertheless is
eagerly looking forward to the next stage – not looking forward to the
actual dying, but genuinely looking forward to drawing closer to God.
The next world is as real to them as this world and they seem to have
one foot in each place – heaven and earth. I know two such people
and they are fun to be with.

And so I tend to think of them when I picture the saint whose
festival we keep today. His name is Polycarp – I know, it's not the
name you would choose to give your baby son these days. He'd have a
terrible time at school with a name like that. It only means 'Much
Fruit' and was a reasonable name to give a child in the first century
when he was born.

He grew up to be a quiet, steady person, not particularly learned
but uncompromising in his preaching of the gospel. And it was a
dangerous thing to preach the gospel in those days. Eventually
Polycarp, who had been a disciple of John, the beloved disciple of
Jesus, was made bishop of Smyrna by his master. Smyrna was a
seaside city of Asia Minor where Homer was supposed to have been
born. By the time Polycarp came on the scene, it was a great Roman
outpost and a centre for the worship of the Roman Emperor and
state. You remember how everyone under Roman rule was supposed
to show that he worshipped Caesar by offering incense and saying
'Caesar is Lord'. This kind of persecution fluctuated. Sometimes the
activities of other religions were ignored or tolerated and Polycarp

had been bishop for nearly fifty years without incident. Then, when he was eighty-six years old, a fresh wave of persecution broke out and there was a popular clamour for the arrest of this lovable old man.

He himself was unmoved by the uproar, but friends persuaded him to seek refuge in the countryside outside Smyrna. He went to a farm to stay with friends but a search party was sent out to arrest him. Eventually they tracked him down and closed in on the farmhouse late at night. Polycarp was in bed in the attic. He could have escaped but refused to do so saying 'God's will be done'. Instead he went downstairs to talk to the police who had arrived, armed to the teeth, to arrest him. The police couldn't help liking this lovable old man and were surprised that there should be such urgency to arrest him. Polycarp asked if he could pray before he left with them and they were content to allow him to do so.

So impressed were they by the sheer warmth and kindness of his character that on their way back they did their best to persuade him to save his own life by conforming to the law, but he quietly replied, 'No, I am not going to take your advice.'

When they reached Smyrna the arena was packed. He was led before the governor who also tried to persuade him to recant. But he would not.

We owe our knowledge of what happened to a man called Marcion, who was actually there at the time. This is what he tells us happened next.

'The Governor, however, still went on pressing him. "Take the oath, and I will let you go", he told him. "Revile your Christ." Polycarp's reply was, "Eighty and six years have I served him, and He has done me no wrong. How then can I blaspheme my King and my Saviour?"'

(*Early Christian Writings*, translated by Maxwell Staniforth, Penguin Books, p. 158)

The crowd continued to yell for his death and a fire was kindled. He was fastened with iron to the pyre and they went to nail him as well but Polycarp said

"Let me be; He who gives me strength to endure the flames will give me strength not to flinch at the stake, without your making sure of it with nails."

So they left out the nailing, and tied him instead. Bound like that, with his hands behind him, he was like a noble ram taken out of some great flock for sacrifice: a goodly burnt-offering all ready for God.'

(Ibid, p. 160)

As he prayed, men set light to the wood and Polycarp was enveloped in flame. Then, says the writer,

'we who were privileged to witness it saw a wondrous sight; and we have been spared to tell it to the rest of you. The fire took on the shape of a hollow chamber, like a ship's sail when the wind fills it, and formed a wall round about the martyr's figure; and there was he in the centre of it, not like a human being in flames but like a loaf baking in the oven, or like a gold or silver ingot being refined in the furnace.'

(Ibid, p. 160)

This is probably the earliest genuine record of the death of a Christian martyr. And you all know the saying, 'The blood of the martyrs is the seed of the church'. Well, today there are about one thousand, four hundred and thirty-three million Christians in the world. Add to that the thousands of millions beyond the grave but alive in Christ and we perhaps begin to glimpse the greatness of the family to which we belong. Polycarp is our older brother in that family, so it is right that we should celebrate his festival today.

Let us pray; Almighty God,
the light of the faithful
and shepherd of souls,
who set your servant Polycarp to be a bishop
in the Church,
to feed your sheep by his word
and guide them by his example:
give us grace to keep the faith which he taught
and to follow in his footsteps;
through Jesus Christ our Lord.

(ASB, p. 855/6, Collect of a Bishop)

Hymn: For all the saints

17. A PAGEANT OF OLD TESTAMENT MOTHERS FOR MOTHERING SUNDAY

Let us pray: Two Readers
Abraham and Sarah
Rebecca and Jacob
Moses' mother and sister
Peninnah and Hannah
Solomon and two women
Rest of class choral speaking

Music: Any cheerful march which opens with a fanfare e.g. Schubert's *Marche Militaire* or any of a number of marches by Sousa.

Fanfare

READER 1 Ladies and gentlemen – we present –
READER 2 A Pageant of Old Testament mothers for Mothering Sunday.

March

Enter Abraham and Sarah

ABRAHAM Sarah, I was ashamed of you. That a wife of mine should laugh at guests!
SARAH I'm sorry, Abraham. I wasn't laughing at *them*. I thought they were laughing at *me*. You know how I've longed for a child. It seemed so unfair that they should say I'd have a child by the time they returned next year – at *my* age.
ABRAHAM Have you forgotten God's promise? – that I shall have many descendants? Is anything too hard for the Lord? When that child is born, we shall call him Laughter as a perpetual reminder that you laughed at God's messenger.
SARAH *If* that child is born, I shall gladly call him Laughter as a perpetual reminder that God gave me great joy by taking away my shame at being childless.

Exeunt

70

READER 1 And when the child was born, he *was* called Laughter. The Hebrew for 'He laughs' is Isaac.

READER 2 Look who's coming now – the mother of twins who was guilty of favouritism – always dangerous in a family. Not altogether her fault though. The elder twin, Esau, had married a couple of foreign girls who didn't know how to treat their mother-in-law and had made life miserable for her. Only human nature, I suppose, to want to get her own back.

Enter Rebecca and Jacob

REBECCA Listen, Jacob. Your father believes he is about to die and is going to give the blessing to the son to succeed him. He has sent Esau out to hunt an animal. I heard him say 'Bring me an animal and cook it for me. After I have eaten it, I will give you my blessing in the presence of the Lord before I die.' Now, my son . . . listen to me and do what I say. Go to the flock and pick out two fat young goats, so that I can cook them and make some of that food your father likes so much. You can take it to him to eat, and he will give you his blessing before he dies. . . .

JACOB You know that Esau is a hairy man, but I have smooth skin. Perhaps my father will touch me and find out that I am deceiving him; in this way I will bring a curse on myself instead of a blessing. . . .

REBECCA Let any curse against you fall on me, my son; just do as I say, and go and get the goats for me.

(GNB, Gen. 27.7–13)

Exit Jacob one way and Rebecca the other

READER 1 And you all know what happened. Isaac was taken in, passed on the blessing to Jacob instead of Esau as he had intended. A sordid tale and yet it shows that God can use even love gone wrong to bring about his purpose.

READER 2 Mothers have their uses in the religious education of their children too. Do you remember Moses' mother?

71

Enter Moses' mother and sister

MOTHER   Stand near the river and watch to see what happens to the baby and then come and tell me.

Exit sister. Mother paces around anxiously. Sister returns

SISTER   Mother, the pharaoh's daughter found him. She has fallen for him – he's like a doll to her. I asked if she would like me to find a nurse to look after him. She seemed pleased. Come on – you'll be paid to look after your own child!

Exeunt

READER 1   And what a vital part his mother was to play in Moses' upbringing. Although he was being brought up at the Egyptian court, learning how men are governed, his mother made sure he learned about the God of his forefathers. On that training was to depend the future history of the Jewish people. And it was entrusted to a mother.

READER 2   Here come two quarrelling women. How much damage is done by the tongue!

Enter Hannah in tears and Peninnah

PENINNAH   Can't think why our husband bothers with you at all. You're useless. *I* give him a child a year. He loves me more than he loves you.

HANNAH   Don't, Peninnah. I know he loves me. He said 'Don't I mean more to you than ten sons?'

(GNB, 1 Sam. 1.8)

PENINNAH   That's not what he said to me. 'Why is she always moping?' he said. 'I can't stand miserable women. No wonder God doesn't regard her as fit to be a mother!'

HANNAH   Don't, Peninnah – please. 'How much longer will you forget me, Lord? For ever? How much longer will you hide yourself from me? How long must I endure trouble? How long will sorrow fill my heart day and night? How long will my enemies triumph over me?'

(GNB, Psalm 13.1–2)

72

Exeunt

READER 1   Hannah's prayer for a child was answered. When Samuel was born his mother was so grateful she took him to the shrine at Shiloh to dedicate him to God. There he stayed to be trained in the Lord's service by the old man, Eli. But Hannah never forgot her tiny son. Each year, we are told, she would make a little coat for him and take it to him when she accompanied her husband to Shiloh.

READER 2   More quarrelling women. What is it this time?

Enter Solomon with two women

WOMAN 1   The child is mine, your majesty.

WOMAN 2   Don't believe her, your majesty. Can't you see that he even *looks* like me?

WOMAN 1   Rubbish. Her child died. This baby is mine.

SOLOMON   Silence, both of you! Bring me my sword. We'll cut the baby in half and you can have half each.

WOMAN 1   Good. A very fair solution.

WOMAN 2   No, your majesty. Don't harm the child. Better that *she* should have him than that the poor mite should die. Give *her* the child.

SOLOMON   That settles it. The child belongs to this woman (indicating woman 2) She has the heart of a mother.

Exeunt

READER 2   High standards they set, the women in Old Testament times even though, on the face of it, they had no rights. We are going to finish with a well-known description of a capable wife.

REST OF CLASS   (*Choral speaking*)

'How hard it is to find a capable wife!
She is worth far more than jewels!
Her husband puts his confidence in her, and he
    will never be poor.
As long as she lives, she does him good and never harm.
She keeps herself busy making wool and linen cloth.
She brings home food from out-of-the-way places, as merchant ships
    do.
She gets up before daylight to prepare food for her family and to tell
    her servant-girls what to do.

73

She looks at land and buys it, and with money she has earned she
    plants a vineyard.
She is a hard worker, strong and industrious.
She knows the value of everything she makes, and works late into the
    night.
She spins her own thread and weaves her own cloth.
She is generous to the poor and needy.
She doesn't worry when it snows, because her family has warm
    clothing.
She makes bedspreads and wears clothes of fine purple linen.
Her husband is well known, one of the leading citizens.
She makes clothes and belts, and sells them to merchants.
She is strong and respected and not afraid of the future.
She speaks with a gentle wisdom.
She is always busy and looks after her family's needs.
Her children show their appreciation, and her husband praises her.
He says, "Many women are good wives, but you are the best of them
    all."
Charm is deceptive and beauty disappears, but a woman who honours
    the Lord should be praised.
Give her credit for all she does. She deserves the respect of everyone.'

(GNB, Prov. 31.10–31)

READER 2   Remember that last line on Mothering Sunday –
            'Give her credit for all she does. She deserves the
            respect of everyone.'

Let us pray: Almighty Father,
            we thank you for our mothers,
            for their loving care and their patience with us.
            When they get on our nerves, help us to be
                patient with them.
            Open our eyes to see that their fussiness
                springs from their love for us.
            Help us not to take them for granted and
            remind us sometimes, especially this weekend,
                to say THANK YOU.

            Hymn: Thank you for every new good morning

74

18. THE ANNUNCIATION – 25 March

Are you awake enough yet to realize what the date is today? It's 25 March. Isn't that exciting? – No? It ought to be. There are about 235 shopping days till Christmas. But perhaps you are not feeling very Christmassy yet. Well, it is time to give the matter some thought because today we celebrate the day when it all began nearly 2000 years ago.

Many of you probably know that one of the few things we *can* be sure about over the birth of Jesus is that it was *not* on 25 December. The date of the celebration was fixed to coincide with a great pagan midwinter festival. It was hard luck in those days when you became a Christian and could no longer in good conscience join in the jollity of the Saturnalia and so Christians began to celebrate the birth of Christ at the same time that their neighbours were enjoying themselves in honour of pagan gods.

Now picture a solemn meeting of learned clergymen. It is probably doing them a grave injustice to laugh at them in this way but it is nonetheless irresistible. Having 'fixed' Christmas they wanted to encourage Christians to remember other events associated with our salvation and, knowing the gestation period of a child to be nine months, they must have worked backwards to today's date. I am sure the Biology staff could give you a more accurate formula than a straight nine calendar months – but, don't forget 25 December makes no pretence to be accurate either. All that really matters is that we remember the great event which Lady Day – the Feast of the Annunciation – today – celebrates. It is the day when Mary said 'Yes' to God.

'And in the sixth month the angel Gabriel was sent from God unto a city of Galilee, named Nazareth, to a virgin espoused to a man whose name was Joseph, of the house of David; and the virgin's name was Mary. And the angel came in unto her, and said, Hail, thou that art highly favoured, the Lord is with thee: blessed art thou among women. And when she saw him, she was troubled at his saying, and cast in her mind what manner of salutation this should be. And the angel said unto her, Fear not, Mary: for thou hast found favour with God. And, behold, thou shalt conceive in thy womb, and bring forth a son, and shalt call his name Jesus. He shall be great, and shall be called the Son of the Highest; and the Lord God shall give unto him the throne of his father David: and he shall reign over the house of Jacob for ever; and of his kingdom there shall be no end. Then said

Mary unto the angel, How shall this be, seeing as I know not a man? And the angel answered and said unto her, The Holy Ghost shall come upon thee, and the power of the Highest shall overshadow thee: therefore also that holy thing which shall be born of thee shall be called the Son of God. And, behold, thy cousin Elisabeth, she hath also conceived a son in her old age: and this is the sixth month with her who was called barren. For with God nothing shall be impossible. And Mary said, Behold the handmaid of the Lord: be it unto me according to thy word. And the angel departed from her.'

(AV, Luke 1.26–38)

Just think for a moment what that 'Be it unto me according to thy word' cost Mary. She was a young girl – probably about the age of our own third years – and the punishment for being pregnant without being married was to be stoned. So, at best, she stood to lose the love and respect of Joseph; at worst, she stood to lose her life. And the choice was hers.

There has been a lot of publicity recently for this Christian doctrine that Jesus was born of a mother who remained a virgin. For some it is an insuperable obstacle and seems ridiculous. I don't suppose anyone has ever been led to Christian faith because of it – quite the reverse – and yet it says in almost shockingly simple terms what Christians believe about Jesus – that he is both God and Man. We too are faced with a choice. If we insist that Jesus had two human parents, then he must have been human, whereas Christians believe that he was God made man. Within the Church you will find wide variations and degrees of faith and doubt. Sit loose to these troublesome doctrines if you can't accept them yet. Over the years they begin to fall into place, but this is a matter of living experience rather than intellectual gymnastics. If you can't yet accept the miracle of the virgin birth, it may help to think of the story as one which tells us something of how God continues to act in the lives of each one of us, though in our case on a less dramatic scale.

God comes to a humble peasant girl and asks her to co-operate with him in giving divine life a human form. Saying 'Yes' will transform Mary's whole existence in ways she cannot at first imagine. There will be suffering. She would stand at the foot of the cross bearing the unendurable pain of watching her dear Son dying in agony. Such was to be her path from poverty in Galilee to being Queen of Heaven. Now, as the angel first speaks to her, she is quite free to say 'No' and get on with her ordinary humdrum existence undisturbed again by whispers from another world. All we know of the way in which God deals with men and women suggests that, had Mary said 'No', God would not have forced her. But Mary said 'Yes' – 'Be it unto me according to thy word' – and so made possible the birth of God made Man. Because Mary said 'Yes' the whole drama of the Incarnation would unfold.

God still asks men and women to co-operate with him in showing forth the life of God in our world today. At baptism we become part of the Body of Christ – here in the world to do his will. And we too are quite free to say 'No' to the lesser demands made of us. Listen to C. S. Lewis describing the later stages of his own conversion,

'The odd thing was that before God closed in on me, I was in fact offered what now appears a moment of wholly free choice. In a sense. I was going up Headington Hill on the top of a bus. Without words and (I think) almost without images, a fact about myself was somehow presented to me. I became aware that I was holding something at bay, or shutting something out. Or, if you like, that I was wearing some stiff clothing, like corsets, or a suit of armour, as if I were a lobster. I felt myself being, there and then, given a free choice. I could open the door or keep it shut; I could unbuckle the armour or keep it on. Neither choice was presented to me as a duty; no threat or promise was attached to either, though I knew that to open the door or to take off the corslet meant the incalculable. The choice appeared to be momentous but it was also strangely unemotional. I was moved by no desires or fears. In a sense I was not moved by anything. I chose to open, to unbuckle, to loosen the reign.'

(*Surprised by Joy*, Fontana p. 179)

Do you see? Once again a choice is offered but complete freedom allowed as to whether the answer shall be 'Yes' or 'No'. It is only because of Mary's first great 'Yes' that God became man at all and so made possible all those more lowly 'Yesses' by which we ourselves are able to draw closer to him. So let us honour Mary and celebrate the day she said 'Yes' to God.

    Let us pray: We beseech you, O Lord,
                to pour your grace into our hearts;
                That as we have known the incarnation of
                  your son Jesus Christ
                by the message of an angel,
                so by his cross and passion

we may be brought to the glory of his
resurrection;
through Jesus Christ our Lord.
(ASB, Collect for the Annunciation, p. 763)

19. PASSOVER – Pesach

You will need:	Two Readers Mother Her two children Israelite father and mother Their two children Moses Variable number of Israelites (five speaking parts) Miriam Variable number of dancers
Props:	Basket containing goods to look like Passover foods, seder plate, candlesticks, cleaning materials, purse with money, bedrolls and bags for ancient Israelites.
Music:	Passover songs

READER 1   We are coming to the time when two of the world's great religions both approach important festivals. Jews are about to celebrate Passover and, for Christians, the events of Holy Week and Easter are not far away. Our assembly today is about Passover and tomorrow we shall think about the Christian celebration of Maundy Thursday.

READER 2   So we begin today with Passover – Pesach to Jewish people. For over three thousand years it has been kept as a great festival of freedom – a time when Jewish people everywhere remember the occasion when God showed his great love for them by leading them out of slavery in Egypt to

78

freedom and a promised land. Even in the darkest periods of their history Jews have never forgotten that time. It is not just something that happened once and for all in the past. It is related to the experience of each one even today. Think of the effect in concentration camps of the closing words of the Seder:

Next year in Jerusalem!
Next year may all be free!
(Living Festivals Series, *Passover* by Lynne Scholefield, p. 30, RMEP)

READER 1   It is a family occasion. Jewish religious festivals are rooted in the home. Everyone has a part to play from the oldest to the youngest but, as usual, it is mother who is mainly responsible for the preparations.

Curtain

Enter Mother with a loaded basket which she unpacks onto the kitchen table

MOTHER   Lamb – horseradish – wine – apples – nuts – cinnamon – salt – eggs – matzoth – parsley. I wonder if I ought to have bought a few more packets of matzoth? Ben's appetite has to be seen to be believed these days and I nearly ran out last year. Perhaps I'd better have some more. Ben! Ben!

Enter Ben

Be a dear and get on your bike. I need three more packets of matzoth. I don't want to run out.

BEN   No! You'd better not! Remember last year and Mrs Isaacs running round scrounging enough to see them through the week? OK. How much will it come to?

MOTHER   (*looking in her purse*) I've only got £5. That's more than enough. Here you are. Watch the change.

Exit Ben

79

Rachel! Come and help me, will you?

Enter Rachel

Would you like to start making the charoseth? Or would you prefer to polish the seder plate and candlesticks?

RACHEL   I'd love to have a go at the charoseth paste. I've only ever helped you with it before. What am I to do?

MOTHER   Pass me over the seder plate and the polish then. I can be cleaning the silver while I'm telling you what do to.

(They settle down to their jobs)

Chop up the nuts. You'll need about eight table-spoonsful. When you've done that, peel one of those cooking apples and grate it into the nuts. Mix it all up. Then add some cinnamon.

RACHEL   How much?

MOTHER   Try about a teaspoonful first and then taste it and see. Then take some of the wine left over from last night and add a little at a time till it's a stiff paste. Pass me over the breadbin. I'd better wash that out. I did the biscuit tin yesterday. We must clear out all the leaven before your father comes home.

RACHEL   Do you remember when Ben and I were small how we used to follow you round with our toy brush and dustpan?

MOTHER   And how excited you got when you found a heap of biscuit crumbs under the piano!

RACHEL   It was years before I realized you used to tip some out ready for us to find. Oh, how I *love* Passover.

MOTHER   Well, you can dig out the copies of the Haggadah when you've finished that. I must get on with preparing the lamb.

Curtain

READER 2   And so, eventually, all is ready. When everyone comes to table, mother lights two candles and everyone follows the words in the service book – the Haggadah. The youngest child asks his father

80

'Why is this night different from all other nights?' and, in answering the child's questions the father retells the whole glorious story of the Exodus from Egypt.

READER 1   Jews really re-live history that night. It is as though each one of them is involved in the events which were first experienced by their ancestors at the time of Moses. And so, now we slip back in time to those days.

Curtain

(Jewish family packing bed rolls and bags ready to leave)

FATHER   They were saying at the brickworks this morning that the boils even spread to the Egyptian cattle.

SON   Yes, and they're still plagued by frogs.

DAUGHTER   And gnats – and flies.

MOTHER   Well, I've seen no sign of any of it round here.

SON   And their river has turned red – like blood. It's quite undrinkable.

FATHER   You heard how the crops were flattened by hail? Well, what was left was destroyed by locusts.

MOTHER   It must be God's doing because we have been spared these plagues round here.

FATHER   Moses seems to know what he is about. You can trust what he says.

MOTHER   But why put the blood of the lamb on the doorpost?

FATHER   It's to be a sign. A sign of our being God's people. Moses says that tonight 'every first-born son in Egypt will die, from the king's own son . . . to the son of the slave-woman who grinds the corn.' (GNB, Exod. 11.5) But the angel of death will pass over our houses because of the blood of the lamb. You can trust Moses. We must just possess our souls in patience now until we see what God intends to do next.

Curtain

READER 2   They didn't have long to wait. As death took its toll 'the Egyptians urged the people to hurry and

81

leave the country: they said "we will all be dead if you don't leave." So the people filled their baking pans with unleavened dough, wrapped them in clothing and carried them on their shoulders.'

(GNB, Exod. 12.33–34)

(Israelite family, loaded, pass across in front of curtain)

READER 1 And the Lord said, 'You must celebrate this day as a religious festival to remind you of what I, the Lord, have done. Celebrate it for all time to come.'

(GNB, Exod. 12.14)

READER 2 The Lord said, 'For seven days you must not eat any bread made with yeast – eat only unleavened bread.'

(GNB, Exod. 12.15)

READER 1 Strictly the Passover story ends there. But their troubles were only just beginning and God was to be with them throughout them all. After endless walking, following God in a pillar of cloud, they came to a great barrier – the Red Sea.

READER 2 Even worse, the Egyptians, realizing they had lost their slaves, were in hot pursuit. 'When the Israelites saw the king and his army marching against them, they were terrified.'

(GNB, Exod. 14.10)

Curtain

(Moses in the lead followed by a rabble of complaining Israelites)

ISRAELITE 1 Weren't there any graves in Egypt? Did you have to bring us out here in the desert to die?

ISRAELITE 2 *(pointing finger offstage to pursuing Egyptians)* Look what you have done by bringing us out of Egypt.

ISRAELITE 3 Didn't we tell you before we left that this would happen?

ISRAELITE 4 We told you to leave us alone and let us go on being slaves of the Egyptians.

ISRAELITE 5 It would be better to be slaves there than to die here in the desert.

MOSES   'Don't be afraid! Stand your ground and you will
         see what the Lord will do to save you today: you
         will never see these Egyptians again. The Lord
         will fight for you, and there is no need for you to
         do anything.'
                                    (GNB, Exod. 14.11–14)

         Exeunt

         Curtain

READER 1 Then Moses held out his hand over the water and
          the sea parted and the Israelites walked on dry
          ground with walls of water on both sides. The
          Egyptians pursued them with horses and chariots
          and drivers – and then it happened – at God's
          command Moses again stretched out his hand
          over the water.

READER 2 And the water returned to its normal level and
          there was no escape for the Egyptians. All were
          drowned.

READER 1 Then Moses' sister, Miriam, took her tambourine
          and all the women followed her playing tam-
          bourines and dancing.

Curtain – Dance

(*Passover song to accompany dancing*)

Miriam sang for them

    Sing to the Lord, because he has won a
        glorious victory
    He has thrown the horses and their riders
        into the sea.
                                    (GNB, Exod. 15.20–21)

Let us pray: . . . let us rejoice
               At the wonder of our deliverance,
               From bondage to freedom,
               From agony to joy,
               From mourning to festivity,
               From darkness to light,
               From slavery to redemption
               Before God let us sing a new song.
               (from the Haggadah quoted in *Passover* by Lynne
                  Scholefield, in the Living Festivals Series, p. 17,
                                                          RMEP)

83

20. MAUNDY THURSDAY

You will need:	Five Readers
	Eight disciples (six speaking parts)
	One king plus retinue
	Almoner (a bishop) non-speaking
	Variable number of elderly people
Music:	*Land of Hope and Glory* (or equivalent) plus fanfare.

Martial music sounds. Enter queen, holding a posy, supported by her retinue. They pass across stage in front of the curtain and exeunt other side.

Fade music sufficiently for reader to speak above it.

READER 1 Today we are remembering Maundy Thursday, the Thursday before Easter. Many of you will have seen on television the ceremony in which Her Majesty the Queen distributes Maundy money to elderly men and women. She goes to a different cathedral each year accompanied by her almoner, the Bishop of Rochester.

Curtain

Elderly men and women gathered in a semi-circle. The Queen accompanied by the bishop passes round the group, handing a small bag to each person in turn. She pauses to speak to each.

READER 2 Those purses contain £5.50 and a set of Maundy money. These coins are specially minted silver pieces representing one penny, twopence, threepence and fourpence and the number of recipients is equal in number to the number of years of the Queen's age.

Close curtain slowly – Fade music

READER 2 The word Maundy comes from a Latin word, *mandatum*, which means 'commandment' and, if you come back in time with us now to the sixteenth century, before the original custom was changed, you will see what the commandment was which Jesus gave us and which now gives its name to Maundy Thursday.

READER 1   It is still Maundy Thursday but this time there is a king on the throne and the scene is Westminster Abbey.

Fanfare. Enter king in procession. Passes across stage as before and exeunt

Curtain

Elderly men and women seated in a semi-circle with bare feet. Enter the almoner with a bowl of water, king now wearing a large apron and a servant with a towel.

READER 2   What on earth is he up to, washing feet? No wonder *that* custom was changed. Why should a king be washing the feet of his subjects? The answer is in St John's Gospel.

(Feet washing continues)

READER 3   'Jesus, knowing that the Father had given all things into his hands, and that he had come from God and was going to God, rose from supper, laid aside his garments, and girded himself with a towel. Then he poured water into a basin, and began to wash the disciples' feet, and to wipe them with the towel with which he was girded. He came to Simon Peter; and Peter said to him,

READER 4   "Lord, do you wash my feet?"

READER 3   Jesus answered him,

READER 5   "What I am doing you do not know now, but afterward you will understand."

READER 3   Peter said to him,

READER 4   "You shall never wash my feet."

READER 3   Jesus answered him,

READER 5   "If I do not wash you, you have no part in me."

READER 3   Simon Peter said to him,

READER 4   "Lord, not my feet only but also my hands and my head!"

READER 3   Jesus said to him,

READER 5   "He who has bathed does not need to wash, except for his feet, but he is clean all over; and you are clean, but not all of you."

READER 3   For he knew who was to betray him; that was why he said "You are not all clean." When he had washed their feet, and taken his garments, and resumed his place, he said to them

READER 5   "Do you know what I have done to you? You call me Teacher and Lord; and you are right, for so I am. If I then, your Lord and Teacher, have washed your feet, you also ought to wash one another's feet. For I have given you an example, that you also should do as I have done to you. Truly, truly, I say to you, a servant is not greater than his master; nor is he who is sent greater than he who sent him." '

(RSV, John 13.3–16)

Curtain

READER 2   Jesus was acting out a parable to underline the teaching he was constantly giving his disciples – that true greatness lies in service. 'You know,' he once said, 'that those who are supposed to rule over the Gentiles lord it over them, and their great men exercise authority over them. But it shall not be so among you; but whoever would be great among you must be your servant and whoever would be first among you must be slave of all.'

(RSV, Mark 10.42–44)

Down the ages our kings and queens have followed his example – first doing literally what he did, but since the seventeenth century doing something more in keeping with modern times.

READER 1   The rest of the events of Maundy Thursday have much in common with Passover, which we thought about yesterday. We must never forget that Jesus was a Jew and his whole way of thinking grows out of the customs of the Jewish people. As a child he would have been the one to ask Joseph 'Why is this night different from all other

86

nights?' and we know that, at the end of his life, he had come up to Jerusalem to celebrate Passover with his friends, knowing that all the elements in the opposition to him were gathering and uniting to destroy him.

READER 2 So now we move once more back in time – to the Garden of Gethsemane on the night of the Last Supper.

Curtain

(*eight disciples sitting huddled in a group*)

THOMAS Quite unreasonable, I call it. I said to him 'How *can* we follow you if we don't know the way?' and now off he goes taking Peter, James and John and telling us to wait here. Doesn't he *want* us to follow him?

SIMON He doesn't seem to realize the danger. I could easily drum up some extra support.

MATTHEW Oh be quiet all of you. I'm frightened, and I don't mind saying so. What did he mean at supper?

PHILIP You mean when he broke the bread and said 'This is my body'?

MATTHEW Yes, and all that business about I AM the Bread of Life

ANDREW It took me back to that day when he fed those 5000 people and we only had five loaves. Yet everyone was satisfied.

NATHANIEL And 'This is my blood of the new covenant'. It gave me the creeps. Sounds like a sacrificial animal. I think he knows he isn't going to live much longer.

ANDREW It reminded me of John the Baptist saying to us when we first saw Jesus 'Behold the Lamb of God'. Peter thinks it's something to do with Passover, but I don't understand what. But look at us now. Jesus asked us to pray and here we are just idly talking.

THOMAS Well I don't *feel* like praying. I'm cold – and tired.

PHILIP Hard luck, Thomas. I'm tired too. We're all tired.

MATTHEW Why don't we pray the prayer he taught us – all together.

87

ANDREW I wish Peter were here.
MATTHEW Well he's not. Stop bellyaching. Come on – pray.
ALL Our Father . . .

(*One by one they fall asleep and the prayer peters out in gentle snores*)

Curtain

READER 1 It's comforting really that even those closest to Jesus let him down.

As we grow in Christian faith, we come to see that the events of Maundy Thursday and Good Friday are a kind of Christian Passover. For Christians, Jesus is the Lamb of God. The ancient Israelites were saved by God through the blood of a lamb. Christians at Holy Communion, when they take the Bread and the Wine, are also saved by the Blood of the Lamb – the Lamb of God – Jesus. You don't have to be very clever to know that what we eat becomes part of ourselves. So the life of God flows into us from the sacrifice of Jesus on Good Friday. And he gave us the sacrament through which that happens at the Last Supper on Maundy Thursday. That's what Maundy Thursday is really all about. So let's celebrate.

Let us pray: Jesus, Lamb of God: have mercy on us.
Jesus, bearer of our sins: have mercy on us.
Jesus, redeemer of the world: give us your peace.

(ASB, p. 143)

And the prayer which Jesus himself taught us:
Our Father . . .

AN END-OF-TERM ASSEMBLY AT EASTER

You will need: | Peter
James
Serving maid
Variable number of soldiers (four speaking parts)
Jesus
Narrator
Pilate
Crowd made up from the audience
Nicodemus
Joseph of Arimathea

Music: | Brahms Symphony No. 4. In scene 1 the opening bars of the second movement will do for cock-crow, interpreting that as the gallicinium.

'I know that my Redeemer liveth' from Handel's *Messiah*.

In the second scene, involve as many people as possible in the crowd. If older teenagers are likely to be disruptive, use the first two years only and group them facing the stage. Be sure to rehearse the shouts of 'Crucify him!' First attempts are likely to be feeble but they soon get the idea!

Music – Brahms Symphony No. 4 first movement – fade

Enter Peter and James in front of curtain

PETER | I don't know what came over me. One moment I was lashing out with a sword and then, before I knew what I was doing, I was running away.

JAMES | We all ran away – (*quietly*) and left him. You're no worse than the rest of us.

PETER | I swore I was ready to die with him.

JAMES | Cheer up! Here we are. John said he could get us into the courtyard so we'll probably find out what's happening.

He knocks. Serving maid emerges through the curtain

89

SERVANT	Oh, it's you – but *two* of you? John only mentioned one. I can't let you both in. The master will notice if there are too many strangers.
JAMES	You go then, Peter. (*To the maid*) My friend can't get a bed anywhere tonight. At least it'll be warm in the courtyard.
SERVANT	It's always the same at Passover – crowds everywhere.
JAMES	See you later then. (*Exit*)

Curtain – Continue music – Fade

Crowd of soldiers standing and sitting round a fire drinking and talking among themselves

SOLDIER 1	Joanna!
SERVANT	Coming, sir! What can I get you?
SOLDIER 2	Uncanny it was. The prisoner just seemed to tower over us all and he's not a particularly tall man. 'I AM' he said and we suddenly seemed powerless to move.
SOLDIER 3	I AM? But that's the divine name – blasphemy.
SOLDIER 2	Blasphemy – or truth. There's something awe-inspiring about that prisoner.
SOLDIER 3	His disciples seem ordinary enough.
SOLDIER 1	Yes, fishermen most of them from all accounts.
SERVANT	(*to Peter*) Aren't you one of them?
PETER	Me? Not me. (*He moves to edge of crowd away from the fire*)

Cockcrow

SOLDIER 3	I'm off-duty now till tomorrow afternoon so I'll push off home now.
SOLDIER 2	You live near Malchus, don't you?
SOLDIER 3	Yes, I'll go in and see how his ear is. (*Exit*)
SOLDIER 2	That's another thing about the prisoner. You'd think he'd've been thankful to have his supporters fighting for him, but he just told them to put away their swords.
SOLDIER 1	Are you still talking about Jesus of Nazareth? I'd heard he was a healer but it still took my breath away when he just touched Malchus' ear and the bleeding stopped. It seemed unreal happening like that before my very eyes.

SOLDIER 4	His friends moved pretty fast when we arrested him. I grabbed one of them but he slipped out of his jacket and ran away naked.
SERVANT	(*pointing to Peter warming himself*) This is one of them.
PETER	I am not. I swear it.
SOLDIER 4	The priests are taking a long time.
SOLDIER 1	They must be short of evidence. He's popular.
SOLDIER 2	He has offended them, though. I was talking to a blind man he healed. You've no idea what a fuss there was.
SOLDIER 1	Why?
SOLDIER 2	He healed on the sabbath and that's against the law.
PETER	But the sabbath was made for man, not man for the sabbath.
SOLDIER 2	Surely you're one of his disciples? You've a Galilean accent.
PETER	I swear I don't know the man.

Cockcrow – Continue second movement quietly

Jesus enters at front. He passes across the stage, hands bound, escorted by soldiers. The crowd falls silent. Jesus turns and looks at Peter who puts his head in his hands and weeps

Curtain

(Fade music. Speakers line up in front of curtain)

NARRATOR	And they led him to Pilate. 'And Pilate asked him,
PILATE	Are you the king of the Jews?
NARRATOR	And he answered him,
JESUS	You have said so.
NARRATOR	And the chief priests accused him of many things. And Pilate asked him,
PILATE	Have you no answer to make? See how many charges they bring against you.
NARRATOR	But Jesus made no further answer, so that Pilate wondered. Now at the feast he used to release for them one prisoner whom they asked. And among the rebels in prison, who had committed murder in the insurrection, there was a man called Barab-

91

	bas. And the crowd came up and began to ask Pilate to do as he was wont to do for them. And he answered them,
PILATE	Do you want me to release for you the King of the Jews?
NARRATOR	For he perceived that it was out of envy that the chief priests had delivered him up. But the chief priests stirred up the crowd to have him release for them Barabbas instead. And Pilate again said to them,
PILATE	Then what shall I do with the man whom you call the King of the Jews?
NARRATOR	And they cried out again,
ALL	Crucify him.
NARRATOR	And Pilate said to them,
PILATE	Why, what evil has he done?
NARRATOR	But they shouted all the more,
ALL	Crucify him.
NARRATOR	So Pilate, wishing to satisfy the crowd, released for them Barabbas; and having scourged Jesus, he delivered him to be crucified.'

(RSV, Mark 15.2–15)

Exeunt

Hymn: There is a green hill

Curtain

Nicodemus and Joseph of Arimathea enter from opposite directions

NICODEMUS	What did he say, Joseph?
JOSEPH	Pilate, you mean?
NICODEMUS	Of course.
JOSEPH	He has given permission and has sent orders to Calvary for the body to be removed. I'm on my way there now with a sheet to wrap it in.
NICODEMUS	Wasn't Pilate surprised that a member of the Sanhedrin should ask for the body of a so-called criminal?
JOSEPH	He knew perfectly well Jesus was innocent.
NICODEMUS	If only I'd had the courage to stand up for him in the Council.

JOSEPH	Me too. I suppose offering the family my own tomb is at least partly to salve my conscience.
NICODEMUS	Do you think they would accept burial spices as a gift from me?
JOSEPH	I'm sure they would. They seemed very pleased to have my offer. But we must be quick. It's only an hour until the Sabbath begins now.

Curtain

| MUSIC: | 'I know that my Redeemer liveth' |
| READER | Who would have thought my shrivell'd heart |

Could have recovered greenness? It was gone
Quite underground, as flowers depart
To feed their mother-root when they have blown;
Where they together
All the hard weather,
Dead to the world, keep house unknown.

These are thy wonders, Lord of Power,
Killing and quickning, bringing down to hell
And up to heaven in an hour;
Making a chiming of a passing-bell.
We say amiss,
This or that is:
Thy word is all, if we could spell.

(George Herbert)

Hymn: Love's redeeming work is done

Let us pray: Almighty Father,
who in your great mercy made glad the disciples
    with the sight of the risen Lord:
give us such knowledge of his presence with us,
that we may be strengthened and sustained by
    his risen life
and serve you continually in righteousness and
    truth;
through Jesus Christ our Lord.

(ASB, Collect for Easter I, p. 602)

93

SUMMER TERM

21. ST GEORGE – 23 April

Tape: 'Once more unto the breach, dear friends' from Shakespeare's *Henry V*, Act 3, scene 1, if possible: otherwise any patriotic music e.g. 'Land of Hope and Glory'.

After the warm humanity of the patron saints of Scotland, Wales and Ireland (see plays in Volume 1) it comes as a shock on St George's Day and Shakespeare's birthday to have to admit that England's own patron saint, St George, may never have existed. Even if he did exist, he wasn't English and never visited these shores. What a let-down! But legends galore have grown up about him and, as you know, legends have a good deal of truth in them even if it is not of the historical or scientific kind. So let's glory in the legends and think what they are trying to tell us.

St George was honoured as a soldier saint. The story goes that our own King Richard the Lionheart was fighting in the Crusades when the English army found itself in a tight corner. King Richard prayed for the help of St George, the captain of the noble army of martyrs, in this battle against the heathen and, to the amazement of his troops – to say nothing of the king himself – a knight in shining armour immediately appeared riding a magnificent horse. On his shield was a red cross on a white background. The soldiers at once realized St George had come to help them and took heart. A great shout went up, 'St George for England!' as they charged into battle. Inevitably victory was theirs but, before the king could thank the knight, the knight had vanished. In recognition of God's help sent to them in their hour of need, King Richard vowed that St George should be the patron saint of England, which he has remained to this very day.

The next time most of us hear about him is in the reign of Henry V. Some of you may have seen the film of Shakespeare's play or be familiar with one of the best-known speeches in the play. The king is cheering his troops into battle at Harfleur.

(*Tape if possible. Otherwise this shortened version*)

'Once more unto the breach, dear friends, once more;
Or close the wall up with our English dead!

In peace, there's nothing so becomes a man
As modest stillness and humility:
But when the blast of war blows in our ears,
Then imitate the action of the tiger;
Stiffen the sinews, summon up the blood,
Disguise fair nature with hard-favour'd rage: . . .
Now set the teeth, and stretch the nostril wide;
Hold hard the breath, and bend up every spirit
To his full height! . . .
Dishonour not your mothers; now attest
That those whom you call'd fathers did beget you!
Be copy now to men of grosser blood,
And teach them how to war! And you, good yeomen,
Whose limbs were made in England, show us here
The mettle of your pasture; . . .
I see you stand like greyhounds in the slips,
Straining upon the start. The game's afoot;
Follow your spirit: and, upon this charge,
Cry – God for Harry! England! And Saint George!'
(*Henry V*, Act 3, scene 1)

So our patron saint is celebrated in our literature. What about the
dragon he killed? That features in another great poem of the English
language – Spenser's *Faerie Queene*, a long poem in seven books. St
George has one whole book to himself. He is called simply the Red
Cross Knight until the day comes when he is granted a vision of the
heavenly city beside which everything else pales into insignificance. A
wise and holy man tells him,

'. . . thou, emongst those Saints whom thou doest see
Shalt be a Saint, and thine own nations frend
And Patrone: thou *Saint George* shalt called bee
Saint George of mery *England*, the signe of victoree.'
(*Faerie Queen*, Bk 1, canto X, Stanza 61)

St George then goes on to fight the dragon which has been terrorizing
the district, leading the king to build a brazen tower in which to hide.
In his jaws

'Threeranckes of yron teeth enraunged were,
In which yett trickling blood, and gobbets raw
Of late devoured bodies did appeare,
That sight thereof bredd cold congealed feare;
Which to increase, and all atonce to kill,

A cloud of smoothering smoke, and sulphure
   seare,
Out of his stinking gorge forth steemed still,
That all the ayre about with smoke and a stench
   did fill.'

(*Faerie Queene*, Bk 1, canto XI, stanza 13)

Lovely gory stuff! Of course the brave knight defeats the terrible dragon. You wouldn't expect it to happen otherwise, would you?

But do stories of a knight killing a dragon have anything to say to sophisticated young men and women in the twentieth century? Only if you are prepared to look beneath the surface. St George's struggle with the dragon is the story of the eternal struggle between good and evil and each one of us is involved in that every day of our lives. We all are called constantly to make choices between right and wrong or between right and less-than-right. And the choices we make determine the kind of people we become. Having St George as our patron saint puts us firmly on the side of right. He *overcame* the dragon remember. How? With courage, yes, but on his shield he had a red cross, the sign of his saviour.

Several centuries before the first references to St George, St Paul, writing from prison to his friends in Ephesus, looked at the Roman soldier standing guard over him and gave a spiritual significance to the uniform he was wearing:

'Put on the whole armour of God, that you may be able to stand against the wiles of the devil. For we are not contending against flesh and blood, but against the principalities, against the powers, against the world rulers of this present darkness, against the spiritual hosts of wickedness in the heavenly places. Therefore take the whole armour of God, that you may be able to withstand in the evil day, and having done all, to stand. Stand therefore, having girded your loins with truth, and having put on the breastplate of righteousness, and having shod your feet with the equipment of the gospel of peace; above all taking the shield of faith, with which you can quench all the flaming darts of the evil one. And take the helmet of salvation, and the sword of the Spirit, which is the word of God.'

(RSV, Eph. 6.11–17)

So, on your way home today, cast an eye upwards to any church towers and you will almost certainly see the flag of St George flying – a red cross on a white background, England's contribution to the Union flag. Then remember the struggle between good and evil and that St George killed the dragon, defended by Christ whose victory on the cross is commemorated on St George's shield and our flag.

Let us pray: As we remember St George of England, we pray,
'Defend, O Lord, your servants with your
heavenly grace,
that they may continue yours for ever,
and daily increase in your Holy Spirit more
and more,
until they come to your everlasting Kingdom.
Amen'

(ASB, Confirmation, p. 257)

Hymn: When a knight won his spurs

22. ST MATTHIAS – 14 May

Today we remember a saint about whom very little is known. His name was Matthias and he was the 'twelfth man' in the team Jesus sent out to do his work after he himself had ascended to heaven. You will remember how important it had been that Jesus had chosen twelve new men to be his disciples – twelve men to form the nucleus of the new people of God in the same way that there had been twelve tribes of Israel forming God's chosen people in the Old Testament.

Judas Iscariot had betrayed Jesus but had come to a sticky end. Matthew tells us he had tried to return the money he had been paid before going out and hanging himself. St Luke, in the Acts of the Apostles, goes in for more gory details. He tells us, 'With the money that Judas got for his evil act he bought a field, where he fell to his death; he burst open and all his bowels spilt out.'

(GNB, Acts 1.18)

St Augustine tried to reconcile these two accounts by suggesting he may have hanged himself, but the rope broke! Does it really matter? Whatever actually happened, the apostles were left one man short and it was Peter who took the lead in arranging to make the number up to twelve.

'Someone must join us,' he said, 'as a witness to the resurrection of the Lord Jesus. He must be one of the men who were in our group during the whole time that the Lord Jesus travelled about with us.'

(GNB, Acts 1.21–22)

97

Notice those qualifications. The man chosen must be able to speak from *personal experience* of the great drama of the resurrection and must have known Jesus during his earthly life. It was very important that the first preaching was based on experience, not hearsay.

Two men were short-listed – Matthias and Justus. The apostles asked God to guide their choice and the lot fell to Matthias. And that is the last time he is mentioned!

But think for a moment of the greatness that was being thrust upon Matthias. Do you remember Malvolio in *Twelfth Night* being conned into believing that Olivia is in love with him? He finds a note planted by those who have suffered from his overbearing conceit, purporting to come from Olivia. The writer praises his yellow stockings and hopes always to see him cross-gartered – in other words, making an exhibition of himself – and Malvolio falls straight into the trap. He dresses himself up in yellow stockings, cross-gartered, and ogles his mistress quoting lines from the letter which he thinks she has written and which has made an indelible impression upon him. 'Be not afraid of greatness . . . some are born great . . . some achieve greatness . . . and some have greatness thrust upon them.'

(Twelfth Night, Act III, scene 4)

So 'some are born great'. We probably think of kings and queens or lords and ladies. You older ones may well have debated whether the House of Lords should be abolished in its present form. Is there any justification for giving someone a voice in government simply because he has inherited a title? But such issues need not bother us in the case of St Matthias. We can be certain his greatness did not come from being high born.

Did he achieve greatness? That begs all sorts of questions. He would probably have been the first to say that *he* achieved nothing. Anything he did achieve was done by *God* working through him. But what do we understand by greatness? Is it fame or fortune? Think for a moment. Your favourite pop star or footballer may well be enormously rich and is undoubtedly famous. But does that make him great? You probably say 'he's great' in the slang sense of the word. But that's not the sense in which Shakespeare or the Bible uses it. A great man, in the conventional sense, is usually someone of outstanding integrity.

So why did I say just now that Matthias had greatness thrust upon him? Well, it was none of his doing. He didn't push himself forward. He wasn't concerned about his own status. The fact that no more is heard about him is in a way typical of great men of God. Do you remember John the Baptist pointing his own disciples away from himself towards Jesus? When the apostles later found themselves so filled with the power of God that they too could heal the sick and restore people to life, they didn't say 'Look at us. Aren't we great?' They pointed to the source of that power – 'in the name of Jesus Christ of Nazareth, I order you to get up and walk!' (GNB, Acts 3.6) says Peter and the lame man does just that.

What else does Malvolio say? 'Be not afraid of greatness.' There are some kinds of greatness we should fear. You all know the saying 'Power corrupts'. If our lofty status makes us arrogant, self-centred and conceited, then we need to fear the effect on ourselves and those around us. But being an apostle of Christ brought a different kind of greatness. When Peter was feeling pleased with himself for following Jesus and said 'Look, we have left everything and followed you,' Jesus replied

'Yes . . . and I tell you that anyone who leaves home or brothers or sisters or mother or father or children or fields for me and for the gospel, will receive much more in this present age. He will receive a hundred times more houses, brothers, sisters, mothers, children and fields – and persecution as well; and in the age to come he will receive eternal life.'

(GNB, Mark 10.28–30)

'Some have greatness thrust upon them.' Those persecutions were real enough and yet 'Be not afraid of greatness'. The apostles were not. Why not? Because they had their master's promise 'I will be with you always to the end of the age' (Matt. 28.20, GNB) and they knew that it was true.

So let's honour St Matthias today – the twelfth man who had greatness thrust upon him.

Let us pray: Lord God, you chose Saint Matthias
to complete the number of the twelve apostles.
By his prayer, include us among your chosen
ones,
since we rejoice to see
that the lot marked out for us is your love.
We make our prayer through our Lord.
(*Divine Office*, *Roman rite*, Prayer on Feast of St
Matthias, p. 149*)

Hymn: For all the saints

99

23. ST AUGUSTINE – 26 May

You will need: Pope Gregory
St Augustine
Variable number of monks
King Ethelbert of Kent
Queen Bertha
Variable number of courtiers
Two Frenchmen
Two Readers

Augustine needs to carry a large cross, and a tape of Gregorian chant is useful though not essential.

READER 1   If you have ever been to Canterbury cathedral you can hardly have failed to notice St Augustine's chair, a huge stone throne which stands all by itself in the centre of the cathedral. It is a constant reminder to us of the saint who made the long journey from Rome for the specific purpose of bringing Christianity to these shores. There were Christians here already, as you will see, but St Augustine's mission did more than anything else to bring about the conversion of the English people.

READER 2   Come with us now back in time to the year 596 and to Rome where Pope Gregory the Great has summoned the prior of his own monastery of St Andrew to see him.

Curtain

(*Pope Gregory seated surrounded by priests talking to him and trying to catch his attention*)

GREGORY   (*rising*) Enough, fathers. I hear Augustine has arrived from my dear monastery of St Andrew. I will deal with these other matters another day. My heart yearns for news of my brethren. Truly I left something of myself behind in that monastery when our Lord called me to be the Servant of the servants of God. Go now, for I see Augustine coming and would speak with him alone.

100

Exit priests one way as Augustine enters from another. Augustine moves to kiss Pope Gregory's ring but finds himself being embraced by the Pope.

GREGORY Brother Augustine! It's good to see you. What news from the monastery? How are my brethren?

AUGUSTINE As eager for news of you as you are for news of them. We pray for you constantly in your high office and thank God for his blessing in allowing us to have had the Holy Father as our own dear father in God for so many years. We miss you, father.

GREGORY Enough of that. I know from my own experience how hard it is to renounce all personal ties for Christ's sake, but we have to remain free if we are to be ready to do whatever our Lord requires.

AUGUSTINE Fortunately he does not require as much from the rest of us as he has required from you.

GREGORY Don't be so sure, my son. I asked you to come and see me for a special reason. I have a difficult mission for someone and am hoping you will undertake it for the Lord.

AUGUSTINE What is that?

GREGORY The conversion of the Anglo-Saxons.

AUGUSTINE You're not serious?

GREGORY Never more serious in my life. A month ago I was passing near the slave market and saw some boys from those shores. Augustine, they were like angels not Angles – messengers sent from God to make us realize that here is a race which must be given the good news of Jesus Christ. There is no one I would rather trust with the task than you. Go back to the monastery. Choose say thirty of the brethren to accompany you and make your way there with all speed. Will you do that for the Lord?

AUGUSTINE Of course, father, if you wish it. But pray for us. In our own strength we cannot possibly succeed.

GREGORY Remember our Lord's words 'Lo I am with you, alway, even unto the end of the world' (AV, Matt. 28.20). Go then, and the Lord be with you.

Curtain – Music

101

READER 2	Augustine chose thirty monks and they set off on foot across France – Gaul, as it was called in those days. The further they went the further their spirits sank into their sandals.

Curtain

Enter Augustine and monks on one side to be met by two Frenchmen approaching from the other side

MONK 1	Excuse me. Are we on the right road for the sea which leads to England?
FRENCHMAN 1	England? You're never going there? They're like wild animals. Some say they have two heads. They attack foreigners on sight. My brother went there and was lucky to get out alive. Hundreds of them came roaring down the shore at them armed to the teeth. He said their battle cry was terrible to hear.
FRENCHMAN 2	That's if you ever reach land. The Anglo-Saxons call the sea the 'whale-road' and invoke the gods of the sea to help them. It is said the storms on that sea are terrible. Waves taller than a house crash down on you and huge fish from below toss your boat into the air. You'll never come out alive.
FRENCHMAN 1	Go back while there's still time.
FRENCHMAN 2	And the food in that country is terrible. They say they eat human flesh – raw!
FRENCHMAN 1	We shall conquer them one day, I'm sure. But go back now. You'll regret it if you don't.
MONKS	Father Augustine, save us!

(*They pull him away*)

Curtain

READER 1	Sheepishly they returned to Rome and Augustine found himself with Pope Gregory.

Curtain

GREGORY	Remember what St Paul suffered, my dear Augustine. 'Five times I have received at the hands of the Jews the forty lashes less one. Three

times I have been beaten with rods; once I was stoned. Three times I have been shipwrecked; a night and a day I have been adrift at sea; on frequent journeys, in danger from rivers, danger from robbers, danger from my own people, danger from Gentiles, danger in the city, danger in the wilderness, danger at sea, danger from false brethren; in toil and hardship, through many a sleepless night, in hunger and thirst, often without food, in cold and exposure.'

(RSV, 2 Cor. 11.24–27)

– and all I ask you to do is sail to England!

AUGUSTINE We heard such terrible tales on our journey our hearts failed us.

GREGORY Would that I could go myself! Would it encourage you to know that I have news from that land that they are well-disposed towards us? From all accounts the king of Kent, whose name is Ethelbert, is a kind and just man. His queen, Bertha, was a French princess and she is a Christian already. Courage, brother!

AUGUSTINE I am ashamed of myself. Bless me, father, for I have sinned. I will go.

GREGORY Go then, and God be with you – and pray for me, also a sinner.

Curtain

READER 2 And so the little band set off again. This time they went the whole way and landed in Thanet. They sent a message to King Ethelbert explaining who they were and why they had come. We go now to the king's court.

Curtain

(*King Ethelbert and Queen Bertha seated on thrones surrounded by courtiers*)

ETHELBERT Of course I'm prepared to see them if it will please my lady. I like that priest you brought with you from Paris and I'll always be prepared to welcome Christians.

BERTHA	Perhaps the day will come when you too will be baptized.
ETHELBERT	That cannot be forced. There's something about the Christians I've met that I like but the gods of my own people have served me well.
BERTHA	Where will you meet Augustine and his companions? Will you invite them here or go to the coast? Wulfstan has a large hall near the beach and would doubtless make it available to us.
ETHELBERT	Not in a hall – out in the open. They may cast spells or use magic if we are indoors.
BERTHA	As you will, my lord. Thank you for welcoming them.

Curtain

READER 1	And so the historic meeting took place.

Curtain

READER 1	King Ethelbert sat under an oak tree surrounded by his courtiers as Augustine, carrying a tall cross, approached and bowed low to the king.
AUGUSTINE	We come in peace, your majesty. This cross is the emblem of the King of Peace whom we serve. With your permission we should like to stay in your beautiful land and tell your people of the joy we know through serving Jesus Christ.
ETHELBERT	I know something of him already. My queen is a Christian and has often spoken to me about Jesus of Nazareth. Yes, you are welcome to stay and convert any who wish to follow your way. On one thing only I insist. No force must be used. The heart can only be freely given.
AUGUSTINE	Such is the way of love, your majesty. God is love and we love him because he first loved us.
ETHELBERT	You shall be well treated. I know too that you will need somewhere to worship. There is a small church in my city which you may use as your own to sing psalms, to pray, to preach and baptize.
READER 1	And so began Augustine's mission to England. A year later on Whitsunday the king himself was baptized and thousands of his followers went the way of their king. So great was their success that

Augustine had to send to Rome for more helpers
and so the conversion of England prospered. So
you see why the Church remembers St Augustine
today.

READER 2 Let us pray:
Father, we pray for all missionaries;
We remember with gratitude those who have
    led us in the path of faith.
We pray especially today for the Archbishop
    of Canterbury.
May the light which St Augustine kindled in
    our land
guide us along the path which leads to Thee.
We ask it in the name of Jesus Christ our Lord.

Hymn: Thy hand, O God, has guided

24. VISIT OF THE BLESSED VIRGIN MARY TO ELIZABETH –
31 May

---

*You will need to think in advance of a place well-known to the
children about eighty miles away from the school.

When did you last visit relations? Is it something you enjoy doing?
Obviously that must depend on which relations. Do you enjoy having
relations visiting you? – even those who say '*How* you've grown!'?
'Aren't you getting like your father!'? Charles Lamb didn't think
much of some of his family. In one of his essays he describes one of
his poor relations who would always contrive to drop in at mealtimes
or when he knew there was likely to be a birthday treat.

'He is known by his knock. Your heart telleth you "That is Mr —." A
rap, between familiarity and respect; that demands, and at the same
time seems to despair of, entertainment. He entereth smiling and –
embarrassed. He holdeth out his hand to you to shake, and – draweth
it back again. He casually looketh in about dinner-time – when the
table is full. He offereth to go away, seeing you have company – but is
induced to stay. He filleth a chair, and your visitor's two children are

accommodated at a side-table. He never cometh upon open days, when your wife says, with some complacency, "My dear, perhaps Mr — will drop in today." He remembereth birthdays – and professeth he is fortunate to have stumbled upon one.'

(Essays of Elia – Poor Relations)

– and so on.

But, if you are lucky, there is likely to be someone in your family with whom you feel completely at home. It may be a cousin of your own age or perhaps a young uncle or aunt or godparent – someone you can talk to in a way that you can't talk to your parents; someone you can trust; someone you know will understand your feelings; someone whose advice you respect.

Well, today the Church is remembering a relationship of that kind and a momentous meeting of cousins. Some people think they may have been aunt and niece as there was a big age difference between the two but they obviously loved and trusted each other. They certainly had plenty to talk about that day.

'Soon afterwards Mary got ready and hurried off to a town in the hill-country of Judaea. She went into Zechariah's house and greeted Elizabeth. When Elizabeth heard Mary's greeting, the baby moved within her. Elizabeth was filled with the Holy Spirit and said in a loud voice, "You are the most blessed of all women, and blessed is the child you will bear! Why should this great thing happen to me, that my Lord's mother comes to visit me? For as soon as I heard your greeting, the baby within me jumped with gladness. How happy you are to believe that the Lord's message to you will come true!"'

(GNB, Luke 1.39–45)

Mary had been given the staggering news that she was to have a child and was to call him Jesus. Do you think she had told her own mother? Or did she want to talk it all over with Elizabeth first?

Don't overlook the geography. When she hurried off to a hill town in Judaea she wasn't trotting up the road and round the corner to the next village. She was walking about eighty miles. That's the distance from here to ***. The archangel who had brought her the message about the birth of Jesus had told her that Elizabeth was six months pregnant, even though she was past the normal age of childbearing, and Mary obviously wanted to share her own news with her cousin and to do what she could to help at the time of the birth of Elizabeth's child.

And then Luke makes it clear that it isn't just the mothers who are bound together by ties of kinship but the two babies are also connected. Elizabeth says 'as soon as I heard your greeting, the baby within me jumped with gladness'. Luke, the doctor, must have known what every mother knows, that by that stage the infant John the Baptist would have been doing a little war-dance in his mother's womb with his tiny feet and elbows kicking much of the time. And Luke, the poet, takes this perfectly ordinary phenomenon and uses it to suggest a link, even before the birth, between Christ and his forerunner.

Even God himself was born into this world as part of a human family with all its ramifications of relationships. What does this tell us? Surely that *none* of us is alone. Even if you are an only child you are part of a wider family. In God's family we are all loaded with relatives because when we acknowledge God as our father everyone else becomes our brother or sister.

At the end of the Anglican baptism service, after the baby or adult has been baptized and adopted into God's family (of which Jesus is the eldest brother) the whole congregation welcomes the newcomer saying

'We welcome you into the Lord's Family.
We are members together of the body of
  Christ;
we are children of the same heavenly Father;
we are inheritors together of the kingdom of
  God.
We welcome you.'   (ASB, Baptism, p. 248)

So today, let's remember Mary and Elizabeth all those years ago rejoicing in God's gift of sons to them. Let's thank God for our own relatives and let's remember that, as we are all children of God, everyone in this school is in one important sense our brother or sister. So let's do our best to make sure that we are a happy family.

Let us pray: Almighty God,
               by whose grace Elizabeth rejoiced with Mary
               and hailed her as the mother of the Lord:
               fill us with your grace
               that we may acclaim her Son as our Saviour
               and rejoice to be called his brethren;
               through Jesus Christ our Lord.
                  (ASB, Collect for the Visit of the BVM to
                                        Elizabeth, p. 831)

Hymn: I belong to a family

107

25. ST BARNABAS – 11 June

You will need:	Two Readers
	Steward
	Two slaves
	Sergius Paulus
	His wife
	Barnabas
	Mark
	Paul
	Peter
	Timothy
	James
	Joseph of Derbe
	Elymas

READER 1 Today is the feast of St Barnabas and we want you to come back with us in imagination to the first century AD and to the island of Cyprus where a banquet is being prepared to celebrate the twenty-fifth anniversary of Barnabas inheriting a large estate from his father.

READER 2 His name hadn't always been Barnabas. That was a nickname given to him by the apostles. It means 'One who strengthens' – gives encouragement to other people and, as you will see, Barnabas was very popular for doing just that.

Curtain

(*Slaves busily putting finishing touches to a long table prepared for a banquet. There are nine places*)

Enter steward

STEWARD Are you nearly ready? Master is expecting Mark to bring the old man in about an hour's time.

SLAVE 1 We *are* ready. Nine places did you say? (*He checks*)

SLAVE 2 I heard the ship bringing the guests had been delayed by storms.

108

STEWARD	No. That was the cargo boat from Perga. Dirty crossing they've had – they still can't get into the harbour. If you go upstairs you can see them bobbing about out there like a cork.
SLAVE 1	Rather them than me. When are the guests from the mainland expected, then?
STEWARD	Oh, they landed some days ago at Salamis. They travelled together from Syrian Antioch and are coming overland. A servant arrived an hour or more ago to say they'll be here by six.

Enter Sergius Paulus

S.P.	Is everything ready, steward?
STEWARD	Yes, master. Barnabas should feel honoured to be received by the governor in this way.
S.P.	It gives me enormous pleasure to have an excuse to honour that man. He transformed my life – he and Paul between them.

(Knock)

Ah – there they are. Go and make them welcome and bring them here.

Exeunt Steward and slaves. Enter S.P.'s wife

My dear – our guests are arriving. All of them agreed to come when they heard what we had in mind. It shows the high esteem in which Barnabas is held that busy men will travel hundreds of miles to join in a celebration in his honour.

Enter Barnabas with Mark

BARNABAS	My lord, I am honoured by your invitation and glad you have included my cousin, young Mark here.
S.P.	We are proud to be able to honour our island's best-loved landowner.
BARNABAS	You make me feel very humble. I've done so little to deserve such words.

(Knocking)

WIFE	Here come the other guests.

(Voices) Enter Peter, Paul, Timothy, James and Joseph from Derbe

(Wife steps forward to greet them)

How glad we are to see you. It's a wild night. You must have had a terrible journey.

BARNABAS Paul – Peter – Timothy, my dear boy – and James – and what news from Derbe? I'd no idea so many of you would be coming. What a wonderful surprise!

S.P. Come, be seated. Barnabas – you take the place on my right. Peter next to my wife.

PETER Paul – come and sit beside me. Remember that time in Antioch when you told me off for trying to avoid eating with Gentiles?

PAUL Shall I ever forget it? In public too! You took it very well.

PETER Not much option. You were right and I was in the wrong.

BARNABAS So was I. It shows how habit dies hard. We'd always been brought up to regard it as wrong to associate with Gentiles and childhood instinct came to the fore. What a revolution you've brought about in our whole way of thinking, Paul.

PETER It makes me cringe to remember my stupidity. Still, you know me – act first, think later. But I should have known better. After all, the Holy Spirit had led me to baptize Cornelius and I'd seen with my own eyes how the gifts of the Spirit had been given to his household.

BARNABAS All that's in the past. Let's forget the idiocies of our youth and rejoice in the common Christian fellowship.

JAMES You were the first to respond to the demands of that fellowship. It was a turning point for our little community in Jerusalem that day you came and shared all the money you had made from selling land on the island. Even the poorest were inspired by your example to share what little they had.

PAUL Little was the word! Do you remember the collection we made in Corinth to help save the Jerusalem community from bankruptcy?

110

BARNABAS   That was after my time, but I heard about it from
            Titus.

            *Enter Elymas, the magician, bowing to Sergius
            Paulus*

ELYMAS   Master, I wonder if I might . . .

            (*he notices Paul, covers his eyes with his arm and
            cringes away*)

            No . . . no . . . spare me . . . I didn't mean any
            harm.
S.P.   Whatever is the matter with you, Elymas?
ELYMAS   That man . . . my sight . . .

            (*he slinks away*)

BARNABAS   You've nothing to fear, my good man.
ELYMAS   That man there (*pointing at Paul*) blinded me
            once.
BARNABAS   I remember. I was here too. But your sight
            returned, did it not?
PAUL   I remember now. He tried to hypnotize me, but
            our Lord saved me by taking away his sight.
BARNABAS   It was hard for him to see two strangers being
            kindly received by his master, particularly when
            one of them seemed to have as much influence as
            you did, Paul.
S.P.   And how grateful I am for that influence. Without
            it I should probably never have known Jesus
            Christ.
BARNABAS   Anyway, Elymas, you needn't worry this time. I
            can promise you it won't happen again.
ELYMAS   All the same, masters, if you'll excuse me . . .
            another time perhaps . . .

            (*He backs away and exits*)

BARNABAS   Tell me your news, Timothy. I was so glad when I
            heard you had joined Paul and Silas in their
            travels.
TIMOTHY   I very nearly didn't. After all, I'd seen what they
            did to you and Paul in Lystra that first time you
            came.
S.P.   What happened?

111

PAUL	We've laughed about it many times since, but it didn't seem very funny at the time.
BARNABAS	There was a cripple there and Paul healed him.
PAUL	*God* healed him, but through me. It was the first time such a thing had happened through me and I was awestruck.
PETER	You shouldn't have been. After all, I told you how *I'd* been allowed to heal a cripple through the name of Jesus.
PAUL	I know. But it's one thing to hear of these things happening through other people – quite another when you yourself are used as a channel for the healing power of Christ.
BARNABAS	The trouble was, the crowds were awestruck too. Decided we were gods and sent for their priests to come and make sacrifices to us.
PAUL	You've never seen anything like it. I looked up and there was this priest coming down the hill with an ox all ready to make a sacrifice to us. Garlands too –
BARNABAS	One for you – one for me.
TIMOTHY	I can see you now, Paul. You rushed into the crowd like a mad thing. Shouting your head off you were. 'We're only human beings like you,' you were yelling.
BARNABAS	The crowd were thoroughly disappointed. Thought there was going to be a fiesta. So he paid the price. They beat him up and left him thinking he was dead. That's when I first met Timothy, though I didn't know your name then, my son. You were a real help to me.
TIMOTHY	My mother had been so impressed by your preaching, she pushed me into coming to help you.
PAUL	When I came to, we were well on the way to Derbe.
JOSEPH OF DERBE	So *that's* why you looked so ill when you arrived in Derbe. I've never heard that story before.
PAUL	Small wonder. You'd hardly expect me to begin my mission in a new town by telling everyone I'd been beaten up in the last place. Barnabas, you were a tower of strength to me then and I shall be eternally grateful.

112

(He stands)

Enough reminiscing. It's time for a toast. But first I must say a brief word about my own personal debt to our dear Barnabas. Truly we named him well – he is indeed one who encourages. I seem confident enough to you all these days, but it hasn't always been so. I was sure enough of myself in the old days before I met our Lord on the road to Damascus. But then I was brought low. It was three years before I had the courage to approach the apostles in Jerusalem when I spent a fortnight there with Peter. Then I kept quiet in Syria for fourteen years. I owe it to Barnabas that I found my place in the church at Antioch. He came to Tarsus and led me back to Antioch where we worked together for a whole year. How I love the Christian community in that place. It is there, after all, that we were first given the name Christian which we are so proud to bear.

BARNABAS *I* was the one who felt proud to have found Paul, the apostle to the Gentiles.

PAUL Yes, I think we made a good pair. Give me your hand, Barnabas. Forgive my ill-temper in refusing to take your cousin Mark with me on that second journey. My life was the poorer for that quarrel. I've already asked Mark's forgiveness and he has been like a dear son to me since.

Cyprus has been the richer for your presence here and we come here today to thank you for all you mean to each one of us. Gentlemen, I ask you to drink a toast to Barnabas.

ALL Barnabas!

(All sing 'For he's a jolly good fellow')

Curtain

READER 1 Let us pray:

Lord God Almighty,
whose Son Jesus Christ has taught us
that it is more blessed to give than receive:
help us by the example of your apostle Barnabas,

113

to be generous in our judgements
and unselfish in our service;
through Jesus Christ our Lord.

(ASB, Collect for St Barnabas, p. 775)

Hymn: For all the saints

26. TRINITY

This is the time of year during which the Church is celebrating the
Trinity – God the Father, God the Son and God the Holy Spirit being
three Persons yet remaining one God. It is a bold teacher who would
embark on the task of explaining the doctrine. All too often such
attempts lead to further confusion. And yet time and again the
questions asked in class indicate that people feel a *need* for the
doctrine even if they do not hope to *understand* it. For example, I
have been asked many times questions like 'Was Jesus talking to
himself when he prayed in the garden of Gethsemane?' or 'If God
made the universe and is looking after it, how could he be looking
after the stars when he was walking round Palestine in the form of
Jesus?'

And it is really the Person of Jesus which makes the doctrine of the
Trinity necessary. You see Christians, like Jews and Muslims, begin
from the firm belief that God is One and that only God is to be
worshipped.

'Hear, O Israel: the Lord our God is one Lord' (Deut. 6.4), says the
Jewish Shema.

'There is no god but Allah, and Muhammad is His Prophet' is the first
Pillar of Islam.

But Christians, as they come to know Jesus, grow in the conviction
that this man is more than man – that he is in fact the living God
himself. And so the Church embarks on walking a tightrope. If you
are not careful you fall for the idea that Jesus was a *man* adopted by
God and raised to the Godhead rather than *God himself* come into
our world as man – made incarnate. Or, going too far the other way, it
is tempting to deny that there is any distinction at all between God
and Christ. But, in that case, you are led to a position of the Father

114

too having been born and died and that runs counter to the teaching of the New Testament.

And so the doctrine of the Trinity evolved and was given its classic statement in the Athanasian Creed: 'The Father incomprehensible, the son incomprehensible: and the Holy Ghost incomprehensible,' says the Book of Common Prayer in words which may well bring a smile to those of us living in the twentieth century.

The point to cling to is that the learned men who evolved this doctrine were only trying to give expression to a fact of common experience. If you walk into the laboratory today and the board is covered with equations your heart may sink. 'What on earth is he on about?' you'll probably think. And then, when the lesson starts, you find you are doing something practical and relatively straightforward. Only afterwards do you discover that all those hieroglyphics on the board are the expression of what you have been doing in your test tubes. 'Give me test tubes every time,' you'll probably think. Or think of a knitting pattern. Have you ever tried an Aran pattern? If you take it stitch by stitch you'll go cross-eyed. But watch a knitter who knows what she is doing. Her fingers will fly. She won't need to read the pattern because she can feel the pattern growing as she goes along.

It's the same with the Trinity. The living experience of Christians makes sense of the doctrine which is impossible if you sit down to confront it with your intellect. You have a mind – the creative part of you. You also have a body which contains all the parts of you and shows you to the world. Above all you have a soul – the part of you which is really you. Your friend doesn't like you because of your brains – he may even be jealous of them. Nor is your beauty the ground of your friendship. It's because you are you that people are drawn to you. Three parts of you but only one, unique, you. There is nobody else in the whole world exactly the same.

It's always dangerous to take a human analogy and say 'Well, God is like that, only much, much greater' and I don't really intend doing so with the doctrine of the Trinity. We are, in the end, the created and cannot expect to understand the Creator. But, because we cannot understand, we must not assume that something does not make sense. It does. The fourteenth century author of *The Cloud of Unknowing* summed it all up when he wrote 'by love He may be touched and embraced, never by thought'.

So, don't switch off in panic at the thought of the Trinity. Live with the idea and celebrate God's glory.

115

Let us pray: Almighty and eternal God,
you have revealed yourself as Father, Son and
  Holy Spirit,
and live and reign in the perfect unity of love.
Hold us firm in this faith,
that we may know you in all your ways
and evermore rejoice in all your eternal glory,
who are three Persons in one God,
now and forever.
(ASB, Trinity Sunday, second collect)

Hymn: Holy, Holy, Holy

27. ST ALBAN – 22 June

You will need:	Two Readers
	Alban
	Variable number of guests
	Two servants
	Amphibulus, the priest
	Variable number of Roman soldiers
	Roman governor
	Court official
Music:	e.g. Handel's *Water Music*

READER 1 Today is the festival of the first martyr to die for the Christian faith in this country. It happened over three hundred years before St Augustine landed at Canterbury, so there were Christians here long before that historic missionary venture.

READER 2 Come with us now back in time to a Roman city in Hertfordshire called Verulamium, to the house of a rich young man called Alban.

Music – Fade

Curtain

(A cheerful crowd of people are taking leave of their host at the end of a party – remains of food on the table)

GUEST 1   A marvellous evening – thank you so much. Goodnight.

ALBAN   Is your carriage there?

GUEST 1   Yes thanks. See you tomorrow in the Forum. Goodnight and thank you again.

GUEST 2   My compliments to your chef – a splendid meal and delightful company. We must get together sometime over that road-widening scheme. Goodnight and a thousand thanks.

ALBAN   Greetings to your family.

GUEST 3   Now, don't forget. We look forward to seeing you this time next week at my house. It has been a lovely evening. Thank you.

GUEST 4   Thank you again. Goodnight.

. . . etc. until everyone has left. Alban, alone, claps his hands to summon servants

Enter servants. They go to clear table

ALBAN   Leave the clearing away until the morning. It is late now and you must be tired. I shall read a while before going to bed but I shan't need you again tonight.

SERVANT 1   *(aside to servant 2)* How lucky we are in our master. I don't know another slave in the city whose master would let him go to bed with work undone.
(To Alban) Thank you, master. You are very kind to us and we appreciate it.

SERVANT 2   What time shall I call you in the morning?

ALBAN   I'll send for you when I wake. There's no hurry for me to get up. Goodnight.

(Knocking)

Who can that be? Someone forgotten something, I suppose. Go and let him in.

Exit slaves. Slave 1 returns

117

SLAVE 1	There's an old man outside. I've never set eyes on him before. He's not a Roman. He looks very tired. Would you like us to give him a meal in the kitchen?
ALBAN	There's plenty of food left here. Bring him up. He can eat here and have a bed for the night if he needs it. It's late to be wandering around the city on his own. He must be in some sort of trouble.

Exit slave returning with old man in priest's clothing

ALBAN	You are welcome, sir. What brings you here at this hour?
AMPHIBULUS	May I speak to you alone?
ALBAN	(*to servant*) Goodnight. You may both go to bed. I can look after our guest.

Exit slave

	(*to Amphibulus*) Come now. Sit up to the table and let's give you something to eat. You look worn out. What's wrong? Can I help in any way?
AMPHIBULUS	God bless you for your kindness. Believe me when I tell you I have done nothing wrong. Please believe that. Because I have to tell you that I am being pursued by enemies who will kill me if they find me, may God forgive them.
ALBAN	What's that you say?
AMPHIBULUS	Truly, I've done nothing wrong.
ALBAN	Then Roman justice will support you.
AMPHIBULUS	I'm a Christian and Roman justice won't support *us*.
ALBAN	But did I hear you say 'May God forgive them' when you spoke of your enemies?
AMPHIBULUS	Indeed you did. They don't understand what they're doing.
ALBAN	I've heard everything now! A man asking his gods to forgive his enemies! Come on. Eat up. Would you like some more wine? You must tell me more about these gods of yours. Are they like the great Jupiter?
AMPHIBULUS	The God I serve died to save those who would destroy him. Let me tell you about him.

118

Alban sits down beside him. Fade in music.
Interlude

Curtain

READER 1   And so, far into the night, the old priest and the young man talked. Amphibulus told Alban how God became man in Jesus, how he died on the cross and rose from the dead and how he was alive in the world and wished all men to share in his divine life through faith in him.

READER 2   Alban was deeply moved – not so much by the priest's words as by the serenity of his nature and by the love which he sensed reaching out towards him. The sun was rising before they finally went to bed.

READER 1   The following evening they dined together alone.

Curtain

(Alban and Amphibulus at table. Suddenly loud shouting is heard)

AMPHIBULUS   *(jumping up)* They're coming. Quick! Where can I hide? God forgive me for bringing trouble on this house.

Loud knocking

ALBAN   God *bless* you for bringing the gospel of salvation to this house. Don't be afraid.

Enter slave breathless

SLAVE   Master! There are soldiers outside. They have a search warrant. They're looking for a Christian priest believed to be hiding in the city.

(Amphibulus crosses himself)

(Slave points an accusing finger) I know that sign! *You're* the Christian! How *could* you bring calamity on my master who has shown you nothing but kindness?
(falls on his knees at Alban's feet) Hand him over, master, I beg of you, or we shall all be killed.

119

ALBAN Quiet! Quickly, father. Give me your cloak. You take mine. Away with you, boy. Keep the soldiers talking as long as you can. Now, father, this way.

(*He pushes him out in the other direction and turns to face the soldiers as they rush in. They surround him, push him roughly to the ground and drag him off*)

Curtain

READER 2 Amphibulus escaped but tradition says he eventually died the death of a martyr.

READER 1 Meanwhile Alban was taken before the Roman governor.

Curtain

(*Governor seated. Alban stands before him guarded by soldiers*)

GOVERNOR Your name?

ALBAN Alban.

GOVERNOR A man of property, I believe.

ALBAN Worldly goods mean nothing to me now. I've found treasure in heaven.

GOVERNOR What nonsense is this? Do you worship Caesar or not?

ALBAN *Not.* I am a Christian. Jesus Christ is the one I serve.

GOVERNOR Now listen. You know the penalty as well as I do. You're young. You're wealthy. All life is before you. Why throw it away?

ALBAN True life is to be with Christ. *Nothing* can separate me from the love of God. 'I am sure that neither death, nor life, nor angels, nor principalities, nor things present, nor things to come, nor powers, nor height, nor depth, nor anything else in all creation, will be able to separate us from the love of God in Jesus Christ our Lord.'

(RSV, Rom. 8.38–39)

GOVERNOR Take him away. Let him die.

OFFICIAL But he's well liked in the town. You may start a riot if any harm comes to him.

GOVERNOR (*shouting*) Take him away, I say!

120

Curtain

READER 1   And so Alban was led away to execution. Legend tells us that the executioner's eyes dropped from his head so that he could not see to wield his axe. This is probably a way of saying that he recognized sheer goodness when he saw it and could not bring himself to destroy it. Another executioner was found and Alban was beheaded.

READER 2   We know that old Roman city of Verulamium as St Albans. A church was built over the spot where he died, to be replaced years later by the magnificent cathedral which bears his name today.

Let us pray: Almighty God,
who called your church to witness
that you were in Christ reconciling men to
    yourself:
help us so to proclaim the good news of your
    love;
that all who hear it may be reconciled to you;
through him who died for us and rose again
and reigns with you and the Holy Spirit,
one God, now and for ever.
(ASB, For the missionary work of the church,
p. 907)

Hymn: For all the saints

28. ST PETER – 29 June

You will need: Two Readers
Peter
Mark
Mary, the mother of Mark
Justus
Rhoda

121

Variable number of Christians
Four soldiers

Music: Background music for a party.

READER 1   Today being St Peter's day, we take you back in time to Mark's mother's house in Jerusalem where a party is in progress to welcome Peter home from his travels.

Music: Voices and laughter behind curtain. Fade music and talk above it

Curtain

An ebullient Peter is in the centre of a laughing, friendly crowd

PETER   OK, Mark my boy. That's enough of mother-in-law jokes. It's a good one, I'll grant you, but I don't feel the same about them these days.

MARK   Why not?

PETER   Didn't I ever tell you about the time the Master healed my Ma-in-law? One Sabbath it was. We'd been in the synagogue and –

MARK   Was that the time he healed the madman?

PETER   That's it. Well, Ma-in-law was at home in bed delirious and my wife was at her wits' end so I asked the Master if he'd come and help her. Just walked in, he did, spoke to her in that quiet firm voice of his and she was right as rain. Got straight up and cooked our supper. Fair took my breath away. You've no idea how ill she'd been. And I've never felt like joking about mothers-in-law since. Anyway, what's the latest about the Zebedees?

(A hush falls. Music stops)

MARY   Haven't you heard?

PETER   Heard what?

MARY   Tell him, Mark.

MARK   You *must* have heard.

PETER   Heard what? What's the matter with you all? You know I've been away – back to Joppa to see Cornelius. Not every day a Roman officer invites

122

a fisherman to be his guest. He'll never forget what happened when I baptized him. Nor shall I!

JUSTUS Not every day the leading apostle baptizes a Gentile.

PETER You're right there, my lad. Proper rumpus it caused here in Jerusalem. But I knew I was right. I don't often have visions but when I do I'm in no doubt. Hey, did I ever tell you what happened when I had a vision of the Master talking with Moses and Elijah? Right fool I made of myself, as usual. James and John were there that day. What's up with them?

MARY Go on, Mark, tell him.

MARK Herod has had James beheaded.

(*Peter covers his face with his hands, totally deflated*)

PETER Out of the depths I cry to thee, O Lord!
Lord, hear my voice!
Let thy ears be attentive
to the voice of my supplications!

ALL If thou, O Lord, shouldst mark iniquities,
Lord, who could stand?
But there is forgiveness with thee,
that thou mayest be feared.

I wait for the Lord, my soul waits,
and in his word I hope;
my soul waits for the Lord
more than watchmen for the morning,
more than watchmen for the morning.
(RSV, Psalm 130.1–6)

PETER Poor Salome. She dotes on those boys. Who's looking after her?

MARY John took her to his house but now he's gone into hiding himself so we're not sure where they are.

MARK You'll need to be careful too, Peter. The authorities are bound to hear you're back.

MARY You're welcome to stay here, of course, but I'm afraid this is the first place they'll look.

(*Loud knocking*)

123

	Who can that be?
VOICE	Open up, in the name of Caesar.
MARK	Police – quick, Peter, hide.
PETER	What's the use? It'll only make more trouble for you. Go and let them in, Rhoda.

Exit Rhoda, returning with four soldiers

SOLDIER 1	We're looking for Peter, son of Jonah.
PETER	I am he. What do you want?
SOLDIER	We arrest you on Herod's orders.
PETER	I'll come with you. Leave these others alone. (*He pauses, smiles at the frightened gathering*) Pray for me, my friends.

Exit Peter with soldiers

MARK	That's just the way the master went that night in Gethsemane. But Peter had the guts to fight for him. Cut off one of their ears in the struggle. Why didn't I do anything to help him tonight?
MARY	There was nothing you could have done, my son. Come now. We must pray for him.
ALL	I cry with my voice to the Lord, with my voice I make supplication to the Lord, I pour out my complaint before him, I tell my trouble before him. When my spirit is faint, thou knowest my way!

In the path where I walk
they have hidden a trap for me.
I look to the right and watch,
but there is none who takes notice of me;
no refuge remains to me,
no man cares for me.

(RSV, Psalm 142 pp. 1–4)

Curtain

| READER 1 | Peter is put in prison. |

Curtain

Peter, seated, guarded by four soldiers

| PETER | Move over. Give a man room to stretch his legs. |

124

	What do you think I'm going to do? – an Olympic sprint out of here?
SOLDIER 1	If you escape, we shall be put to death.
SOLDIER 2	And we know you have magic powers.
PETER	If you believe that, you'll believe anything.
SOLDIER 3	They say that if even your shadow falls on someone sick he is healed.
SOLDIER 4	And I saw with my own eyes that cripple that used to beg by the Temple jumping and prancing about. That was some years back now. You healed him, didn't you?
PETER	Not exactly. He was healed in the name of Jesus of Nazareth. You crucified him but he rose from the dead. It was faith in Jesus the Christ that cured that cripple.
SOLDIER 2	I said you had magic powers. What on earth do you mean by rising from the dead? Things like that don't happen.
PETER	I've seen it with my own eyes. Ate breakfast with him afterwards on the shores of Lake Galilee. I'd let him down badly. Promised him I was ready to die for him and then, when the crunch came, denied him three times over. But he forgave me and trusted me. I'll never forget that day. He made me a new man.
VOICE	There's to be *no* talking to the prisoner. That's an order. Do you hear?
4 SOLDIERS	Sir!

Curtain – slowly

READER 1	'Suddenly an angel of the Lord stood there, and a light shone in the cell. The angel shook Peter by the shoulder, woke him up, and said,
READER 2	Hurry! Get up!
READER 1	At once the chains fell off Peter's hands. Then the angel said,
READER 2	Fasten your belt and put on your sandals.
READER 1	Peter did so, and the angel said,
READER 2	Put your cloak round you and come with me.
READER 1	Peter followed him out of the prison, not knowing, however, if what the angel was doing was real; he thought he was seeing a vision. They

passed by the first guard post and then the second, and came at last to the iron gate leading into the city. The gate opened for them by itself, and they went out. They walked down a street, and suddenly the angel left Peter.

Enter Peter, bemused, in front of curtain

PETER   Now I know that it is really true! The Lord sent his angel to rescue me from Herod's power and from everything the Jewish people expected to happen.'

(GNB, Acts 12.7–11)

He crosses the stage and knocks on the door of Mark's mother's house. From behind the curtain voices can be heard praying

VOICES   Deliver me from my persecutors;
for they are too strong for me!
Bring me out of prison,
that I may give thanks to thy name!

(*Rhoda opens the door*)

the righteous will surround me;
for thou wilt deal bountifully with me.

(RSV, Psalm 142.6b–7)

(*Rhoda shrieks with delight, slams the door leaving Peter outside and a confused babble of voices is heard from behind the curtain. Peter continues to knock.*)

Curtain

Everyone greets him warmly. Handshaking, back-slapping. Fade in music. Party resumes.

Curtain

READER 2   Let us pray:

We pray today for all leaders of the church;
for all who bear the name Peter
and for ourselves –
'As to Peter in the waste of waters,
stretch forth thy hand and hold us up,

126

calm thou the storm without,
within be thou our peace.'
(*A Pilgrim's Book of Prayers* by Gilbert Shaw,
p. 36, SLG Press)

Hymn: For all the saints

29. ST THOMAS THE APOSTLE – 3 July

Today we celebrate the feast of St Thomas – doubting Thomas – that forerunner of Christians all down the ages who find the call to faith more than they can cope with. We do him less than justice if we see him as one of those who say 'Prove to me that Jesus is God (or nowadays more likely 'that there *is* a God') and then I'll believe'. The world is full of such people and there must have been millions of them over the centuries. But they miss the point. Where there is no room for doubt there is no need for faith, and so we are denied the opportunity of showing God that we trust him. *He* knows, but we need to exercise that trust if it is to grow.

You remember the story of Thomas and his doubts. On the evening of the first Easter Day the disciples were hiding behind locked doors expecting at any moment to be arrested themselves as followers of Jesus of Nazareth who had been crucified three days earlier. There were rumours that he had been seen alive. Women had gone to the tomb and claimed to have seen him. But you can't believe all that women say! More disturbing, Peter thought he'd seen him too. Sad about old Peter. The strain of the past week had obviously been too much for him and he must have been seeing things. Made him hopping mad, though, if you greeted his tale with the suggestion that he should go and have a good sleep. Then there were those two who had come rushing back from Emmaus with a cock and bull story of a stranger on the road who turned out to be Jesus before vanishing from the supper table. Things like that just don't happen. Obviously they all needed a good break. Then – suddenly – Jesus stood there with them. They were amazed beyond belief – overwhelmed, terrified and joyful all at once. Were there murmurs of 'I told you so'? – or were they swallowed up in awe?

127

Now, were they seeing a ghost? Was it wishful thinking? If you ever talk about religion at all, you must know the argument. It goes something like this. 'You believe because you want to believe. You can't face life on your own. You've invented a god to keep you company. I'd rather stand on my own two feet knowing there's nothing and no one there and having the courage to say so. At least I'm being honest.' All very commendable but those are not the arguments of a doubting Thomas. They lack one essential ingredient – experience of the friendship of God.

You remember that Thomas wasn't there that evening. When the others told him about it he said, 'Unless I see the scars of the nails in his hands and put my finger on these scars and my hand in his side, I will not believe.' (GNB, John 20.25b) That demand for certainty springs from loyalty to Jesus. There was nothing Thomas would have liked better than an encounter with the risen Christ. He *knew* him. He missed him. He wanted him with all his heart. But it all seemed too good to be true. It was the disciples' reliability he doubted, not Jesus. And then he is given the chance of a lifetime.

A week later the disciples were together again indoors, and Thomas was with them. The doors were locked, but Jesus came and stood among them and said, 'Peace be with you.' Then he said to Thomas, 'Put your finger here, and look at my hands; then stretch out your hand and put it in my side. Stop your doubting, and believe!'

(GNB, John 20.26–27)

And what does he say? 'My Lord and my God.' *Doubting* Thomas is the first person after the resurrection to say that Jesus is God. And that is the Christian faith – that Jesus is God. Thomas is a Christian with doubts, not someone asking for proof before trying Christianity. There's all the difference in the world. We all have doubts. Grappling with them helps us to grow. But we are only doubting Thomases if we have made that first leap of faith towards Jesus and no one can do that for us. People can tell you about his friendship. They may share some of the fruits of that friendship with you, but he doesn't want our friendship at once removed.

I have a cousin in Australia. You can't see her. I can't prove to you that she exists. I might show you some of her letters. You can say you don't believe she wrote them. I might ring her up and talk to her. She might ring me. You might still say you don't believe she exists and there's really not much I can do about it. But supposing she rings *you*? Will you lift the receiver? If you don't and still insist she doesn't exist, you're not a doubting Thomas, you're a fool. If you do, you'll

128

probably like the sound of her, might even want to get to know her better. There will probably be things about her you doubt – but you've made contact. *That*'s like doubting Thomas. But remember, the first step is to lift the receiver.

Let us pray: Almighty and eternal God,
who, for the firmer foundation of our faith,
allowed the apostle Saint Thomas to doubt the
    resurrection of your Son
till word and sight convinced him;
grant to us, who have not seen,
that we also may believe
and so receive the fullness of Christ's blessing;
who is alive and reigns with you and the Holy
    Spirit,
one God, now and for ever.
(ASB, Collect for feast of St Thomas the Apostle,
p. 785)

Hymn: Let all the world in every corner sing

30. ST BENEDICT – 11 July

You will need:	St Benedict Nurse (non-speaking) Variable number of students Four rowdy monks Six–eight monks to read parts of the Rule Two Readers
Tapes:	(i) cheerful student songs e.g. Brahms' *Academic Festival* overture (ii) Monks singing plainsong – there are a number of excellent recordings by Benedictine monks.
READER 1	Our story this morning is about a drop-out who became a saint and it starts in Rome around the year 500.

129

Student music

Curtain

A crowd of students drinking, back-slapping, cheerful. Enter Benedict. He pauses. The crowd stares and then he joins in with them

Fade music sufficiently for reader to speak above it

READER 2   A young man is enjoying the life of a student in the great city of Rome. His parents are rich. He can afford almost anything he wants – please himself – and that is exactly what he intends to do.

Music up

Friends gather – drinking – talking

Curtain

READER 2   Time passes and the young man, Benedict, gradually comes to feel the emptiness of a life given over entirely to pleasure without reference to God.

READER 1   He is saddened by the gulf between rich and poor and by the selfishness of those with the money to do as they please. One day he packs up and leaves Rome.

Enter Benedict, pack on back. He crosses in front of curtain and exits the other side. He is followed by his devoted nurse, old now but still trying to look after him. She mimes an enquiry to the reader who points her the way Benedict has taken.

READER 2   After many adventures Benedict went out into the countryside to a place called Subiaco having decided to lead the life of a hermit. He persuaded a friend to lower him to a cave below a hillside where no one could reach him and there he stayed, cared for by the friend who lowered food to him – a loaf a day.

READER 1   The complete drop-out. He too lived in a time of wars and threats of wars and this was his response. Maybe we can learn from his experience.

READER 2   We move now to a community of monks not far
            from Benedict's hermitage.

            Curtain

            A group of monks quarrelling

MONK 1   I did it yesterday. It's your turn to wash up.
MONK 2   I won't. I've been here longer than you.
MONK 3   Be quiet, both of you.
MONK 4   Well I cooked the meal so I'm not washing up.
MONK 3   Brothers! Brothers! We can't go on like this. Did
            not the Lord say 'How good and pleasant it is for
            brothers to dwell in unity?' Listen to me.
MONK 4   Why should we?
MONK 2   Someone must take the lead and I've been here
            longest.
MONK 1   Well, I'm not prepared to be ordered around by
            you.
MONK 3   Brothers! Brothers! Listen. None of us is fit to
            lead. We need a new beginning. I'd like to ask the
            hermit of Subiaco to come and teach us the way of
            God.
MONK 2   Well, if you won't have me, even though I have
            been here longest, I suppose the only thing is to
            find someone from outside.
MONK 1   I agree. Who'll go and ask him?
MONK 3   I know a friend of his. I'll have a word with him.
MONK 4   Agreed! Go at once and God be with you.

            Curtain

            *Monk 3 emerges in front of curtain, walks thought-
            fully across the stage and returns with Benedict*

            Curtain

            *Monks assembled. Benedict enters and blesses
            them. All line up and exit chanting.*

            Plainsong

            Curtain

            (Fade music)

READER 2   However, these monks were not used to discipline
            and didn't take kindly to it at all. In fact they were

                              131

not our idea of what monks should be like at all. The story goes that they tried to poison Benedict but that the cup broke as he put it to his lips. So you will often find pictures of St Benedict have a cup on the ground beside him with a wide crack showing.

READER 1 Benedict returned to his cave and the life of a hermit. Then something began to happen. News of his wisdom spread throughout the area and disciples came seeking his advice. Gradually he established monasteries in the area and himself became superior of one of them. Eventually however he left Subiaco and moved to the great hill south of Rome now called Monte Cassino where he established the mother house of the Benedictine community.

READER 2 It was here that he wrote his famous Rule which eventually led to his becoming known as the Father of Western monasticism.

Curtain

Benedict seated writing, speaking the words aloud as he writes

BENEDICT Therefore must we establish a school of the Lord's service; in founding which we hope to ordain nothing that is harsh or burdensome.
(*Rule of St Benedict* – Prologue, translated by Justin McCann, Sheed & Ward)

Enter one by one the monks named. Mime according to the part of the Rule being read

ABBOT Let the abbot when appointed consider always what an office he has undertaken and to whom he must render an account of his stewardship; . . . let him study rather to be loved than feared. Let him not be turbulent or anxious, overbearing or obstinate, jealous or too suspicious, for otherwise he will never be at rest. Let him be prudent and considerate in all his commands. (*Rule*, ch. 64)

PORTER At the gate of the monastery let there be placed a wise old man, who understands how to give and

132

receive a message and whose years will keep him
from leaving his post. (*Rule*, ch. 66)

CELLARER As cellarer of the monastery let there be chosen
out of the community a man who is prudent, of
mature character, temperate, not a great eater,
not proud, not headstrong, not rough-spoken, not
lazy, not wasteful . . . let him not vex the brethren.
(*Rule*, ch. 31)

A JUNIOR AND A SENIOR The juniors, therefore, shall honour their
seniors, and the seniors love their juniors. In
addressing one another let them never use the
bare name; but let a senior call his junior
'Brother', and a junior call his senior 'Nonnus',
which signifies 'Reverend Father'. (*Rule*, ch. 63)

CRAFTSMEN If there be craftsmen in the monastery, let them
practise their crafts with all humility, provided the
abbot give permission. But if one of them be
puffed up because of his skill in his craft, supposing that he is conferring a benefit on the monastery, let him be removed from his work and not
return to it, unless he have humbled himself and
the abbot entrust it to him again. (*Rule*, ch. 57)

GUEST MASTER (*entering with a guest*) Let all guests that come be
received like Christ, for he will say: I was a
stranger and ye took me in. (*Rule*, ch. 53)

CELLARER It is with some misgiving that we determine how
much others should eat and drink. . . . We do,
indeed, read that wine is no drink for monks; but
since nowadays monks cannot be persuaded of
this, let us at least agree upon this, to drink
temperately and not to satiety. (*Rule*, ch. 4)

ABBOT Above all, let not the vice of murmuring show
itself in any word or sign, for any reason whatever. (*Rule*, ch. 34)

BENEDICT Whoever, therefore, thou art that hastenest to thy
heavenly country, fulfil first of all by the help of
Christ this little Rule for beginners. And then at
length under God's protection, shalt thou attain
those aforesaid loftier heights of wisdom and virtue. (*Rule*, ch. 73)

Curtain

133

Plainsong

READER And so the Rule of St Benedict has been passed down to us through the centuries. Its strength lies in its insistence on balance. Life is to be lived in the presence of Christ, whether the disciple is doing the work of God in the chapel or in the kitchen. Earlier in his life Benedict had advised a monk who had chained himself to a rock in an excess of penitential zeal to bind himself with the chains of Christ rather than with those of iron. And that is sound advice for each one of us.

Let us pray: Almighty God,
by whose grace St Benedict,
kindled with the fire of your love,
became a burning and a shining light in the
  church;
inflame us with the same spirit
of discipline and love
that we may walk before you
as children of light;
through Jesus Christ our Lord

(ASB, Collect of an abbot)

Hymn: For all the saints

LEAVERS' ASSEMBLY

The last assembly of the school year is bound to produce mixed feelings. We are all looking forward to the holidays and yet the shadow of parting falls over us. Some of you, I am sure, have been looking forward to this moment for years. And it is right that you should be looking forward. I've never agreed with that old chestnut about schooldays being the happiest days of your life. Of course we hope you have enjoyed your schooldays, but it would be a calamity if for the rest of your lives you were to feel that all the best things were in the past. I don't believe for one moment that that will be so.

There are two things I want to say to you. First, I would like to suggest to you that leaving school is the *beginning* of learning, not the end of it. There's something rather sad about making a bonfire of all your books as a celebration of this day. I remember a young man being urged by his family to throw away his old chemistry notes. The family were moving to a smaller house and were trying to make a clearance. He couldn't bring himself to do it. Not that he would ever need the information again but, not being a scientist by nature, the information in those files had been acquired by the sweat of his brow and those notes had come to represent the process by which he had learned *how* to learn. I'm not suggesting you should never throw anything away – far from it – but hope you will have come to value learning during your time here and that you too will have learnt *how* to learn. It is something you will need to do for the rest of your lives. Cato started to learn Greek when he was eighty years old. I wonder what plans for new learning *you* will have in sixty years' time?

Secondly, I want to remind you of an old story. There was once a village approached by a long, winding country lane. Wending their separate ways along this lane came two travellers, perhaps a mile apart. As the first traveller neared the village, he met a man coming in the opposite direction. He greeted the villager and asked him what kind of people lived there.

'What kind of people live in the place whence you come?' came the reply.

'The best you'd ever find on earth,' replied the traveller. 'They are friendly, helpful and kind. You'd never be lost for a helping hand or a kind word there.'

'That's what you'll find in this place,' said the villager, 'friendly, helpful and kind people. You'll never be lost for a helping hand or a kind word in this place either.'

'Thank you,' said the traveller and continued his journey cheerfully.

Then the second traveller approached and, meeting the villager, enquired what kind of people lived in the village.

'What kind of people live in the place whence you come?' asked the villager.

'Proud, hypocritical, back-biting and mean,' answered the traveller. 'I didn't like any of them.'

'I'm sorry,' replied the villager. 'You'll find they're just the same here; all of them proud, hypocritical, back-biting and mean.'

'What is the world coming to?' grumbled the second traveller and went on his way scowling.

135

Think about that story. Other people's attitudes to us may well be a reflection of our attitude to them.

There will always be a welcome for you here. We enjoy hearing of your doings – conventional and unconventional – so let us have news of you sometimes. Don't feel you can only come back if you have covered yourselves with glory. Each one of you has given something to the school and each one of you matters to us. All of you take with you our prayers and best wishes for the future.

Let us pray: Lord as we thank you for the blessings of the past
and offer you ourselves in the present,
we pray for your guidance in our future.

May the grace of our Lord Jesus Christ . . . etc.

Hymn: Lord, dismiss us with thy blessing